COMPLICIT

Complicit

How We Enable
the Unethical and
How to Stop

Max H. Bazerman

PRINCETON UNIVERSITY PRESS

PRINCETON AND OXFORD

Requests for permission to reproduce material from this work should be sent to permissions@press.princeton.edu

Published by Princeton University Press
41 William Street, Princeton, New Jersey 08540
99 Banbury Road, Oxford OX2 6JX

press.princeton.edu

Library of Congress Cataloging-in-Publication Data

Names: Bazerman, Max H., author.
Title: Complicit / Max H. Bazerman.
Description: Princeton : Princeton University Press, [2022] |
    Includes bibliographical references and index.
Identifiers: LCCN 2022013107 (print) | LCCN 2022013108 (ebook) |
    ISBN 9780691236544 (hardback) | ISBN 9780691236551 (ebook)
Subjects: LCSH: Business ethics. | Ethics—Psychological aspects. |
    Corporations—Corrupt practices. | BISAC: BUSINESS & ECONOMICS /
    Business Ethics | PHILOSOPHY / Ethics & Moral Philosophy
Classification: LCC HV6768 .B39 2022 (print) | LCC HV6768
    (ebook) | DDC 364.16/8—dc23/eng/20220324
LC record available at https://lccn.loc.gov/2022013107
LC ebook record available at https://lccn.loc.gov/2022013108

British Library Cataloging-in-Publication Data is available

Editorial: Joe Jackson, Josh Drake
Jacket Design: Karl Spurzem
Production: Erin Suydam, Lauren Reese
Publicity: James Schneider, Kate Farquhar-Thomson
Copyeditor: Anne Healey

This book is dedicated to the scholars most central to my understanding of ethics:

Mahzarin Banaji

Dolly Chugh

Joshua Greene

David Messick (deceased)

Don Moore

Ann Tenbrunsel

CONTENTS

This is the third book that I have written on ethics. My friend and coauthor Ann Tenbrunsel and I published the first, *Blind Spots*, in 2011. *Blind Spots*, based on collaborative research that Ann and I did between the mid-1990s and 2010, made an early contribution to the literature on the psychology of why good people often do bad things without their own awareness. *Better, Not Perfect*, published in 2020, moved in a more prescriptive direction, offering insights into how we can overcome barriers to behaving ethically. The book took many, many years to write, as I continually encountered relevant ideas from philosophy about which I needed to learn more. The timing of *Complicit: How We Enable the Unethical and How to Stop* was very different. At the time of the 2020 U.S. presidential election, I had no idea that I might write a book on complicity. A year later, the full book was drafted and had been read by many friends and colleagues. The book was inspired by the stunning and outrageously complicit behavior of so many people that culminated in a coup attempt threatening American democracy on January 6, 2021. How could so many people willingly play a role in allowing this coup attempt to happen?

As I started to learn the answers, I was struck by parallels among complicitors in so many of the most harmful events that have occurred in recent years. While I expect that most readers will not identify with the complicitors whom I describe

in chapters 2 and 3, I am confident that readers will identify with many of the complicitors who follow these early chapters. I include my own role in multiple episodes of wrongdoing, including an extended case in chapter 7, to highlight the ubiquity of complicity.

ACKNOWLEDGMENTS

I spent the majority of my career studying the topics of decision-making (now often called behavioral economics) and negotiation. Both of these subject matters often run up against ethical issues, which increasingly interested me. And I have been surrounded by a large number of incredible colleagues who have helped me transition from decision-making and negotiation to the topic of ethics. Mahzarin Banaji, Dolly Chugh, Joshua Greene, David Messick, Don Moore, and Ann Tenbrunsel have all been core to providing me with the insights that were needed to be able to write *Complicit*.

I tend to get consumed with whatever project is currently on my desk. Thus, many colleagues and friends have experienced my obsession with complicity while I have been writing this book. I appreciate their tolerance, their disagreements with me, and their stories. I also shared earlier versions of the book with a number of friends and colleagues. Their insights sharpened my thinking, helped me avoid errors, and deepened what I think I now know about complicity.

I have had the great fortune to advise many scholars who have moved on to amazing scholarly careers. This group includes Modupe Akinola at Columbia University, Dolly Chugh at the Stern School at New York University, Kathleen McGinn at the Harvard Business School, Katy Milkman at the Wharton School, Don Moore at the Haas School at Berkeley, and Todd Rogers at the Harvard Kennedy School of Government. All six

of them took time away from their own busy schedules to read (or, in Don's case, listen to) an earlier draft of their book. They have all improved the document that is now in your hands.

My most critical reader, once again, was my spouse, Marla Felcher. Marla has sensibilities that I lack and offers sharp guidance on where my writing has gone off the rails. I really appreciate her inputs, even when we are arguing about them. Linda Ginzel, Mike Tushman, Eric Eyre (author of *Death in Mud Lick*, a fascinating book about complicity in the opioid crisis), Elizabeth Sweeny, Mark Steitz, and anonymous reviewers for Princeton University Press all read part or all of earlier drafts and played important roles in making the book better. Dr. Kathryn Reed, an OB/GYN physician at the University of Arizona, took to attending executive programs at Harvard in the last few years and along the way became my friend and critical reader of my recent books. Joe Jackson, my editor at Princeton University Press, helped me through a series of wise decisions. And, as always, Katie Shonk, my personal editor, improved the ideas and most of the sentences throughout the book. To the extent that you find the book easy to read, you and I have Katie to thank for that.

Many of my books have been coauthored. At other times, as when writing *Complicit*, I became obsessed with a topic that was best written about on my own. Still, what I know about ethics has been profoundly affected by my colleagues and coauthors. There are dozens of others whose ideas have shaped how I think about ethics, complicity, and related topics. Learning from this broad and amazing community of friends has been a joy. Thank you for all of your insights.

1

The Complexities
of Complicity

In 2004, as the opioid crisis was taking off in the United States, McKinsey, the global management consulting firm, began selling advice to Purdue Pharma on how to increase sales of its opioid drug OxyContin. McKinsey's work for Purdue continued until 2019, many years after Purdue pleaded guilty in 2007 to misbranding the drug and opioid addiction had become a devastating national epidemic. In 2021, McKinsey agreed to a $573 million settlement with forty-seven U.S. states for working to help "turbocharge" Purdue's sales efforts.[1] "Early in their relationship," the State of California argued, "McKinsey advised Purdue that it could increase OxyContin sales through physician targeting and specific messaging to prescribers."[2]

During many of the years that McKinsey was advising Purdue on how to boost sales of OxyContin and evade government regulation, the drug-regulation division of the U.S. Food and Drug Administration (FDA) was paying McKinsey to offer advice on how to strengthen its regulation of pharma, among

other topics. McKinsey's contracts with the FDA required it to disclose such obvious conflicts of interest. But in 2021, after ProPublica asked the FDA for documents related to any such disclosures filed by McKinsey, the FDA turned up nothing "after a diligent search of our files."[3]

Even after news of McKinsey's work enabling Purdue's wrongdoing became public knowledge in early 2019, the FDA continued to seek advice from McKinsey. Between February 2019 and January 2021, McKinsey received more than $2.0 million in new FDA contracts.[4] McKinsey's dual role in advising the FDA and Purdue clearly worked against the public interest. In 2008, after the FDA told Purdue that it planned to require the company to submit a drug-safety plan for OxyContin, Purdue tasked McKinsey with devising a response to the agency. McKinsey proposed options in a PowerPoint presentation that included suing the FDA or banding together with other opioid producers—some of which were also McKinsey clients, including Johnson & Johnson and Mallinckrodt Pharmaceuticals—to fend off new FDA regulations. When Purdue chose this latter path, McKinsey helped implement the strategy, including preparing Purdue executives for meetings with FDA officials. Around this time, the FDA paid McKinsey to develop a "new operating model" for the office developing drug-safety plans. In 2012, the FDA issued a "substantially watered-down" version of the opioid-safety plan, according to ProPublica.[5]

In 2013, with its FDA contracts ongoing, McKinsey recommended a number of specific sales tactics to Purdue, including focusing sales calls on high-volume opioid prescribers, pushing higher and larger (and therefore more lucrative) dosages, and trying to distribute OxyContin directly to patients and pharmacies. In 2017, McKinsey advised Purdue on how to incentivize pharmacies to write more and higher-dosage OxyContin

prescriptions that would actually capitalize on addiction. For example, McKinsey recommended that Purdue offer large bonuses (nearly $15,000) to pharmacies like CVS when one of their patients developed an addiction or overdosed on the opioid.[6] "McKinsey was using its immense talents to help Purdue Pharma sell more pills, and it worked," North Carolina attorney general Josh Stein, one of the leaders of the 2021 settlement with McKinsey, told the *Washington Post*. "The number of pills prescribed, Purdue's profits and McKinsey's fees all skyrocketed, but so did the number of people addicted, the number of people overdosing, and the number of lives lost."[7] Even as McKinsey worked with opioid companies to boost their sales, it continued to advise the FDA, other government groups, and nonprofits on how to abate the crisis.

In 2018, when the state of Massachusetts sued Purdue over its role in the opioid crisis, McKinsey went into panic mode. Two McKinsey senior executives discussed destroying documents relating to the firm's opioid work.[8] But, as is common when McKinsey is found complicit in the wrongdoing of its clients, the firm itself did not admit to culpability in the opioid crisis. Kevin Sneader, the global managing partner of McKinsey, issued a bland statement in response to the settlement: "We chose to resolve this matter in order to provide fast, meaningful support to communities across the United States. . . . We deeply regret that we did not adequately acknowledge the tragic consequences of the epidemic unfolding in our communities. With this agreement, we hope to be part of the solution to the opioid crisis in the U.S."[9]

McKinsey bills itself as "the trusted advisor and counselor to many of the world's most influential businesses and institutions."[10] The firm protects itself legally by insisting that its consultants only make recommendations and leaves decisions

up to the client. In other words, after paying McKinsey millions of dollars for advice, the client is free to reject that advice. Yet in recent years, McKinsey has moved into the business of helping its clients implement its suggestions. This is exactly what McKinsey did with Purdue, Colorado attorney general Phil Weiser told the *New York Times*: two McKinsey senior partners worked with members of the Sackler family, Purdue's principal owners, to put its plans in place, even overruling Purdue executives. "When you see the actions of these McKinsey partners, they were almost acting as executives of the firm," Weiser told the *Times*.[11] Despite its involvement in Purdue's day-to-day decisions, McKinsey attempted to avoid taking real responsibility for its role in the opioid crisis.

As we will see in chapter 8, Purdue is far from the only client that McKinsey has helped commit wrongdoing for profit. And while its willingness to pay $573 million in penalties may be unusual, McKinsey is not the only advisory firm that has helped clients create harm.

Helping others engage in wrongdoing is not unique to famous consulting firms, of course. Many of us face decisions about whether to be complicit in others' unethical behavior, including whether to work for companies that are destroying the environment, deceiving customers, selling inferior products, or creating inequity in the world. Sometimes we assist in less damaging areas of an organization's business; sometimes we help the wrongdoer commit harm more directly. I am not a lawyer, and I offer no legal advice in this book. But as a behavioral ethicist, I can offer guidance on whether we are complicit when others are likely to use the help we give them—whether they pay for it or not—to create harm.

By describing McKinsey's role in the opioid epidemic, I do not mean to let Purdue Pharmaceuticals and the Sackler family

off the hook. As we will see in chapter 2, there is plenty of blame to go around. And, as you will read, other complicitors helped Purdue lead so many pain sufferers to become addicted to OxyContin and overdose. The consultants, distributors, pharmacies, and prescribing physicians involved all should have considered their roles in allowing the opioid epidemic to develop. Looking at stories you may have previously read about from a different perspective, *Complicit: How We Enable the Unethical and How to Stop* will show that complicitors *always* surround the most famous evildoers.

My Complicity—and, Perhaps, Yours

I often face decisions about which corporations I should provide my teaching and consulting services to. Some of these calls are not hard: I would readily decline to work with Exxon, given how the company intentionally distorted the climate change debate to boost its profits.[12] Similarly, my personal ethics would lead me to decline to work with companies in the meatpacking, tobacco, and gun industries. But I also teach in multiple open-enrollment executive programs at the Harvard Business School. How should I respond when executives from organizations that I would not work with show up as my students? I believe I have an obligation to welcome them as I would any other student. After all, that is the implicit agreement I make when I agree to teach in these programs. But perhaps I am complicit by passing along effective negotiation and decision-making strategies to executives who may use them to do work that I consider to be unethical. Does the fact that I try to teach them to audit and improve their ethical behavior help my case? I will explore my own complicity throughout this book, including in an extended story (chapter 7) that I mentioned in the preface.

We have all witnessed people engaging in behaviors that we believed to be wrong, behaviors we would never engage in ourselves. Did we speak up or take steps to stop unethical acts? When we see someone being harassed, do we speak up and protect them? When a colleague tries to give their advisee or friend an advantage in a hiring decision, do we bring their bias to the attention of the rest of the group? When our division's financials don't make sense, do we push for clarity until they do? When our organization sets the low bar of doing what is legal rather than what is right, do we argue for a higher standard? When a not-for-profit provides potentially misleading data to its donors, do we make the dishonesty clear? More broadly, when we don't stand up in the face of dishonesty, are we complicit in it? I am confident that you could add to this list of questions, based on your own uncomfortable experiences with complicity.

Most of the stories that I will share in *Complicit* focus on the business sector. Some will come from the political world and from academia. In all of these stories, too many people were complicit in the unethical behavior of others. These stories will focus on those who enabled Adam Neumann (WeWork), Elizabeth Holmes (Theranos), the Sackler family (Purdue Pharma), and many of the most notorious sexual predators of our time, including Harvey Weinstein (Miramax and the Weinstein Company). You will be familiar with some of these stories. But, in contrast to past accounts of these stories, *Complicit* will focus on the overlooked importance of others who were complicit in the bad behavior. You will learn about the people who distributed the opioids created by the Sackler family, the venture capitalists who ignored the impossibility of WeWork's business model, Walgreens's decision to bring Theranos's fraudulent technology into its stores, and leaders who looked the other

way when they should have stood up to perpetrators of sexual assault. In short, you will look at familiar stories in a new light.

As we will see, complicity can impose huge costs on all spheres of society and across eras: from the rise of Adolf Hitler in Nazi Germany; to the assault on our democracy by Donald Trump and his supporters; to the ethical, financial, and legal crises that plague too many of today's organizations—including, possibly, your own. We will also explore the psychology of why people collaborate with harm doers, as well as how we can become less complicit. Writing *Complicit* has helped me think about my own past complicity with unethical behavior. I hope it will help me be less complicit in the future by prompting me to think about these issues in a more deliberative manner. And I hope that reading the book will help you do so as well.

What We Know about Improving Ethics

Many histories of teaching ethics date back to Socrates. While Socrates authored no texts, he is known through the posthumous accounts of his students, including Plato, who went on to mentor Aristotle. The philosophical traditions established by Socrates, Plato, and Aristotle have now had an extraordinary influence on scholars' thinking about ethics for almost 2,500 years. During these two and a half millennia, philosophers dominated the dialogue about ethics and often focused their debates on establishing what constitutes the most ethical behavior possible.

One perspective from philosophy that speaks to the ethicality of complicit behavior is utilitarianism.[13] Utilitarian philosophers argue that an action is ethical when it maximizes value for all. Some utilitarians define this as maximizing pleasure and minimizing pain for humans. Philosopher Peter Singer explicitly

includes all sentient beings. According to utilitarians, when you help a company engage in behavior that allows it to make more money but imposes far greater harm on other parties, such as people who suffer from the company's pollution or customers harmed by its products, that behavior is not ethical. From a societal perspective, the harm that Purdue and McKinsey inflicted by promoting excessive opioid use far outweighed the positive value generated by reducing pain and helping these companies profit.

Interest in ethics outside of the philosophical community increased dramatically at the start of the twenty-first century with a series of high-profile corporate scandals, including the fall of energy company Enron. In the years since, there has been no shortage of news stories about very bad people who created massive harm in the world, many of whom I will discuss in this book. These early twenty-first-century scandals put pressure on business schools to take the topic of ethics more seriously, especially since many of the leading villains had earned degrees from top business schools. Before 2000, ethics was not core to the business school curriculum. That has changed dramatically over the last two decades. And while ethics was primarily the domain of philosophers for 2,500 years, the scholars teaching and researching ethics in business schools in the new century tend to be behavioral scientists who created a new field: behavioral ethics. In a departure from the philosophical study of ethics, which focuses on how people should behave, behavioral ethics focuses on identifying how people actually behave. This marked a shift in focus from the normative study of ethics to a descriptive approach. I was a part of this evolution, and I documented my specific views and research on ethics in *Blind Spots*, my 2011 book with Ann Tenbrunsel.[14] This book attempted to shine a light on the many ways in which generally good people act unethically without their own awareness.

Another interesting transition concerns whom the new behavioral scientists chose to study. While much of the motivation to study and teach ethics came from stories about wrongdoers such as Kenneth Lay, Jeff Skilling, Bernie Madoff, Jeffrey Epstein, and the like, behavioral scientists soon pivoted away from these "bad apples" and instead focused on the surprisingly frequent bad behavior of ordinary people. Research in this area, which came to be known as "bounded ethicality," reveals that many of us frequently engage in unethical behavior without conscious awareness. For example, studies on bounded ethicality found that many people discriminate based on ethnicity and gender without any awareness of their bias and that we often fail to notice the harm that groups we belong to create.[15] Related to the concept of bounded ethicality is the idea that humans have "bounded awareness."[16] That is, we often fail to notice and use easily accessible, perceivable, and useful information in our decision-making. I will explore the psychology of how our bounded awareness can keep us from fully noticing wrongdoing and lead us down the path of complicity. Overall, the direction taken by behavioral scientists has been very fruitful in developing insights that could help others become more ethical.

One reason we focused on the unethical actions of ordinary people is that we lacked insight into how to improve the behavior of the most famous harm doers. In *Complicit*, I argue that we may have pivoted away from these prominent episodes of harm too quickly. While I readily admit that I know little about how to reform the worst members of society, I believe we left an important opportunity behind, one I return to in this book. We may not know how to deter the truly evil from engaging in their actions, but—by stopping those around them from enabling and participating—we can halt their actions. Those

who create great harm always depend on the complicity of ordinary people. This book examines how we can stop being complicit in wrongdoing, taking the needed fuel of social support away from those who want to do massive harm.

Within the field of ethics, complicity is far from a new topic. In the thirteenth century, Thomas Aquinas listed nine ways in which we might be complicit: by command, by counsel, by consent, by flattery, by receiving, by participation, by silence, by not preventing, and by not denouncing.[17] Notably, Aquinas explicitly includes complicity that occurs through acts of omission (that is, by silence, by not preventing, and by not denouncing). By contrast, contemporary philosopher Christopher Kutz's complicity principle focuses on how people facilitate harm created by others by purposely participating in their wrongdoing or harm.[18] Consistent with Aquinas's broader view, we will discuss complicity as evolving from inaction as well as from action. More important, the profiles that I develop do not emerge from an analytic structure borrowed from the philosophy literature on ethics[19] but rather from a descriptive account of the ways in which humans in contemporary society are complicit in the harms inflicted by others.

One common criticism of philosophical writing about ethics is that it is too demanding, setting a high moral bar that is nearly impossible to reach.[20] Too often, people reject philosophical arguments on ethics because the sacrifices required to be ethical appear too great. In the current context, it is unrealistic to expect that any of us can fully avoid complicity. I certainly do not think that I can completely avoid being complicit with creating harm for the rest of my life. But I do believe that by deliberating about my own complicity, I can dramatically reduce the degree to which I will facilitate wrongdoing in the future. I hope that this book can provide similar guidance for you. To

refer back to the title and main theme of my prior book, *Better, Not Perfect*, I hope that *Complicit* can make us better, even if it doesn't make us perfect.[21]

Making Sense of Complicity

I define "complicity" as being involved with others in an illegal or unethical activity or wrongdoing. My definition of complicity overlaps with the more controversial terms "collaboration" and "enabling." Complicity implies an act that creates net harm. This is not necessarily the case for collaboration and enabling, which can be done for good. However, collaborating sometimes describes cooperation with an enemy. And enabling also sometimes describes what happens when we allow or encourage someone else, often someone we care about, to continue a destructive pattern of behavior. I will most often use the term "complicity" in this book, but because the negative definitions of collaborating and enabling overlap, I will use them at times. Another note is that while "complicitor" is not a word in most dictionaries, it is often used in legal contexts. I use the term to define those who are complicit in the harmful action of another party. Finally, both complicity and harm occur on a continuum. I will use terms related to "harm" throughout this book, including "evil," "wrongdoing," and "harmful behavior." I will generally save the word "evil" for the most extreme cases.

In the next seven chapters, I will tell stories of harm doers who depended on seven different but complementary profiles of complicity in their followers. These profiles form the core of the book, as they allow us to audit our own behavior and consider how we can avoid our own complicity in the future. In all likelihood, some of these profiles will appear to be about people who are very different from yourself, committing wrongs that

you would never dream of committing. But I am confident that most readers will see at least glimpses of themselves in other profiles (particularly the latter ones)—I know that I do.

Each profile will narrate, in some depth, several episodes that exemplify a type of complicity. Within each profile, we will meet primary harm doers and identify and explain the complicity that surrounds them, and then delve briefly into the psychology that underlies the behavior of the complicitors.

Part I of the book includes the harsher and most obvious forms of complicity, "true partners" and "collaborators." Many readers will not personally identify with these two profiles, yet I expect you may recognize the behavior of people you know. Most complicity in these first two categories is explicit and intentional. We will then move on in part II to five profiles of "ordinary complicity," or types of complicity that many of us engage in, often without our deliberative consideration of the harm we are enabling. Psychologists Mahzarin Banaji and Tony Greenwald use the term "ordinary prejudice" to describe the ways in which we favor some groups of people over others, outside of our conscious awareness and control.[22] I borrow their use of "ordinary" to describe the behavior of regular people who allow harm to develop as a result of their implicit, non-deliberative behaviors. I predict that among these profiles of complicity, most readers will recognize themselves. These profiles cover those who benefit from privilege, those who are true believers, those who defer to authority and loyalty, those who rely on their trust of others, and those who create and accept unethical systems.

These seven profiles overlap, and many stories of harm doers include complicitors from multiple profiles. These profiles also vary in the degree of responsibility that complicitors should feel for their inaction or action. I hope that this taxonomy of

forms of complicity gives you ideas for reducing complicity in the future, as it has done for me.

In part III, we will integrate our understanding of all the profiles and the psychology behind them to come up with solutions. In those chapters, we will address the important question of how we can become more aware of the risk of complicity and consider ways to encourage others to avoid becoming complicit when they witness or suspect wrongdoing.

Obvious Complicity

True Partners

Between 1999 and 2019, nearly 247,000 people died of prescription opioid overdoses in the United States.[1] Roughly the same number of people died of overdoses from illicit opioids, including heroin and fentanyl, during the same period. In 2015 alone, the nation lost more than $500 billion to the opioid crisis, measured by lost productivity and taxpayer funds spent on health care, law enforcement, care for children of addicts, and other costs.[2] The opioid epidemic was driven by the pursuit of profit at the expense of the suffering of others. One organization, owned by one family, was responsible for intentionally leading millions of Americans into chemical dependency that, predictably, led to hundreds of thousands of deaths. Purdue Pharma, owned by the Sackler family, made billions of dollars by creating and (mis)marketing the pain medicine OxyContin. As we'll see, Purdue had many true partners in creating the massive harm that resulted.

The history of Purdue's (mis)marketing of OxyContin dates to the 1950s, long before the company began selling the drug.[3] Arthur M. Sackler was a Renaissance person: a psychiatrist,

hospital administrator, patron of the arts, and advertiser. "No single individual did more to shape the character of medical advertising than the multi-talented Dr. Arthur Sackler," declared the Medical Advertising Hall of Fame in 1998.[4] "His seminal contribution was bringing the full power of advertising to pharmaceutical marketing." In fact, what Sackler did was sell his marketing services to pharmaceuticals firms to lend their products a false "patina of science." He taught them how to best misrepresent scientific evidence to their financial advantage and how to radically influence doctors through so-called pharmaceutical detailing by offering bogus speaker's fees and free travel, meals, and samples. Sackler also launched journals that gave preferential treatment to biased research from his consulting clients. All these practices were designed to increase the number of prescriptions that doctors would write rather than to guide them toward optimal medical advice.

In 1952, Arthur and his two brothers, Raymond and Mortimer, who were also psychiatrists, purchased a small pharmaceutical firm, Purdue Frederick, that earned about $22,000 in annual revenue at the time. After Arthur Sackler died in 1987, his family sold off their stake in the company to Raymond and Mortimer, and its name was eventually changed to Purdue Pharma. The company began testing OxyContin as a potential pain medication in the early 1990s, and the FDA approved the drug in 1995. Arthur's descendants would later try to separate his name from the opioid scandal, given that he passed away before OxyContin existed. They also claimed to be appalled by Purdue's "deceptive marketing."[5] But Purdue applied Arthur's marketing insights to sell the drug and hired IMS, the pharmaceutical data and marketing firm he cofounded, to gain insights into doctors' prescribing habits. As Arthur had in the past, Purdue created physician "education" programs to

provide misleading and incomplete scientific evidence about OxyContin.

A couple of features of OxyContin, Purdue Pharmaceuticals' brand-name version of the extended-release form of oxycodone, made it susceptible to fueling the opioid epidemic. First, oxycodone is a powerful pain drug. Like morphine and heroin, its core ingredient comes from opium plants. Morphine, heroin, and oxycodone are physically and psychologically addicting narcotics. Second, the drug's extended-release feature—denoted by the "contin" in OxyContin—made it more dangerous. The core benefit of extended-release pain medication is that chronic pain sufferers only need to take a pill twice a day; immediate-release medication requires more frequent use. With an extended-release product, Purdue was able to get the FDA to allow pills to include far more active ingredients than an immediate-release drug because—if used as directed— they would be released over a longer time period. However, OxyContin developed a huge following of users who had no intention of using it as directed. To disarm the time-release action of the medication and achieve a quick and powerful high, abusers could crush a tablet and ingest or snort the powder, or dilute a pill in water and inject it. This type of misuse produced a euphoria akin to that of heroin, along with a similar danger of overdose. This misuse contrasts with responsible medical use, which would weigh the short-term pain relief that OxyContin provided against the product's downsides, including suppression of the respiratory system, sedation, constipation, nausea, and, most important, addiction and abuse.[6]

After its launch in 1995, OxyContin jump-started the opioid epidemic, becoming the drug of choice for those most likely to abuse an opiate. While OxyContin may well have been a very useful drug for late-stage cancer patients in severe pain, for

whom addiction was not a concern, it was a poor choice for many others suffering from chronic pain. When OxyContin users would try to stop using the drug, many suffered intense and painful side effects of withdrawal. Far too many became addicted and overdosed. Some people who ended up on workers' compensation due to a work-related injury never returned to work, often because they had become addicted to opioids.

The challenge, as defined by Purdue in the late 1990s, was how to expand the market for OxyContin, increase patients' usage levels, and fend off concerns about abuse. It did this through a series of misleading actions. First, Purdue consistently claimed that the risk of addiction from OxyContin was extremely small. Purdue trained its salesforce to claim, unsupported by any objective evidence, that the risk of addiction was "less than one percent."[7] Purdue also consistently claimed that time-release products were less attractive to addicts than immediate-release products, given that addicts wanted an immediate high rather than a gradual effect from the drug. The problem was that addicts knew how to misuse the drug to release a much larger payload up front, such that it packed a more powerful and highly addictive punch. Yet Purdue's salesforce was trained to convey the false message that "Delayed absorption, as provided by OxyContin tablets, is believed to reduce the abuse liability of the drug."[8]

Starting in 1996, Purdue executives regularly received information that OxyContin pills were being crushed and snorted, stolen from pharmacies by desperate addicts, and being prescribed by unethical doctors who knew the pills would be abused. Yet Purdue continued to falsely market OxyContin as less prone to abuse and addiction than other prescription opioids. On multiple occasions, three top Purdue executives—president Michael Friedman, chief legal counsel

Howard Udell, and chief medical officer Paul Goldenheim—claimed they first became aware of the increased risks of OxyContin abuse in 2000. But federal prosecutors found the words "street value," "crush," and "snort" in 117 internal notes between 1997 and 1999.[9]

In 2006, based on a multiyear investigation, federal prosecutors recommended that Purdue as a company and Friedman, Udell, and Goldenheim as individuals be indicted on felony charges, including conspiracy to defraud the U.S. government. If convicted, the executives could have gone to prison. "The Indictment charges a multi-object conspiracy with the overall goal of maximizing the revenues from the sale of OxyContin through fraud, deceit, and false statement," as well as lying to Congress, wrote Kirk Ogrosky, deputy chief of the fraud division at the U.S. Department of Justice, in a memo.[10] For reasons that remain unclear, the top officials in the Department of Justice during the George W. Bush administration did not support this recommendation. Instead, they settled the case on terms much more lenient to the company and its executives. Specifically, in 2007, Purdue and the three executives pleaded guilty to a charge of "misbranding" OxyContin by misrepresenting its risk of addiction and potential to be abused.[11] Purdue and the executives paid a combined $634.5 million in fines; the executives were sentenced to probation and community service. Friedman agreed to pay $19 million of the total fine, Udell paid $8 million, and Goldenheim paid $7.5 million.

As Purdue's actions were being examined by regulators, legislators, and the courts, the company focused its attention on how to influence politicians. Richard Blumenthal, the attorney general of Connecticut, Purdue's home state, highlighted his concerns about the drug company's overly aggressive marketing, both to Purdue CEO Richard Sackler and to the media.

In response, Robin Hogen, Purdue's chief spokesperson, left a voicemail message on the phone of one of Blumenthal's assistants:

> I want to signal our very high level of disappointment in the way the whole press was handled around the A.G.'s comments on this Medicaid fraud. . . . I thought we had an understanding he was going to clarify and retract the statements last night. . . . Purdue Pharma is a significant supporter of the Democratic Party. . . . I think there is an election coming up, and I can assure you that this has not helped his cause in this camp.[12]

In 2020, Purdue reached an $8 billion settlement with the Department of Justice and pleaded guilty to three felony counts, including conspiracy to defraud the United States and two counts of conspiracy to violate the Federal Anti-Kickback Statute. The settlement did not release the company's executives or owners from criminal liability. In 2022, after lengthy legal battles and negotiations, the Sacklers finally reached a deal with most U.S. states and the District of Columbia to help them address the damage caused by the opioid crisis. The Sacklers agreed to pay $6 billion and to release confidential documents detailing Purdue's lobbying, public relations, and marketing activities. They also attended a hearing in which people whose lives were ravaged by opioid addiction had a chance to confront them about their role in the crisis. The Sacklers negotiated immunity from current and future civil claims against them, though criminal prosecution remained a possibility.[13] While Purdue has filed for bankruptcy, the Sacklers will remain among the wealthiest people in the world.

Purdue executives Michael Friedman, Howard Udell, and Paul Goldenheim, along with many other leaders and

employees of Purdue Pharmaceuticals, were undoubtedly complicit in the opioid epidemic that made many of the Sacklers
enormously wealthy while killing hundreds of thousands of
people and ruining many families and communities. But the
complicity extends far beyond the Purdue organization and
the Sackler family. For someone to get hooked on OxyContin,
if they weren't stealing it or buying it from street dealers, one or
more physicians would need to continually prescribe the drug
to them, and a pharmacy or hospital would have to provide
them with the drug. In *Death in Mud Lick*, his investigative
account of the opioid crisis in West Virginia, Pulitzer Prize–
winning journalist Eric Eyre exposes the complicity of physicians, pharmacists, and distributors in the epidemic.[14]

The term "pill mill" describes an office or clinic where
powerful narcotics are prescribed or dispensed inappropriately or for nonmedical reasons. Because federal law prohibits
doctors from prescribing pain medication without a legitimate
medical purpose or for purposes outside of their medical practice, many pill mills are disguised as pain-management centers.
Eyre tells the story of Dr. Donald Kiser, who lost his license to
practice medicine in West Virginia on charges of trading prescriptions for sex. So, Kiser set up a pill mill in Marietta, Ohio,
170 miles away. "The move to Ohio didn't slow down Kiser's
business," writes Eyre.[15] About once a week, Kiser sent a van
to pick up "patients" in West Virginia and drive them free of
charge to Marietta. Kiser paid the drivers in pills, which the
drivers sold on the black market. Kiser wasn't an isolated case.
For many physicians, the profits to be gained from selling prescription opioids, accompanied by little actual medical advice,
was too attractive of a proposition.

Sav-Rite in Kermit, West Virginia, was one pharmacy that
was complicit in the opioid crisis. Located in a coal-mining

region, the tiny town of Kermit was particularly hard-hit by the crisis. Its citizens were prone to back injuries incurred in the mines, and poverty and despair plagued the area. Kermit's population was just 209 in 2000, according to the U.S. Census, and the town is distant from any significant population center. Yet in 2005, the small-town pharmacy Sav-Rite dispensed an average of 54,000 opioid pills a day, all from physician-written prescriptions. People traveled many miles to wait in long lines at Sav-Rite's takeout window for their prescription. While they waited, people illegally resold drugs in the parking lot. Many other pharmacies became well known among OxyContin users for their lax approach to filling prescriptions.

Opioid's Distributors: Purdue's Implicit Partners

Please take a moment to write down the names of firms that you think are likely among the largest twenty firms on the 2020 Fortune 500 list.

If you thought of Walmart, Amazon, Exxon, and Apple, you did well, as these are the top four. You might have also thought of Ford, General Motors, and AT&T, which made the list. It is less likely that you thought of McKesson, which came in at number eight, AmerisourceBergen, which placed tenth, or Cardinal Health, listed at number sixteen. These are three health-care distribution companies, or what have historically been described by the (sexist) term "middlemen." They don't make any products, and they don't sell to customers; rather, they move products along the distribution system. Specifically, Cardinal Health, McKesson, and AmerisourceBergen distribute more than 90 percent of America's prescription drugs and medical supplies. In another astounding statistic provided by Eyre, between 2008 and 2015, these three distributors shipped over

twenty million prescription painkiller pills to just two pharmacies located four blocks from each other in West Virginia.

The U.S. government's Controlled Substances Act puts the legal burden on distributors to flag and report suspicious orders from pharmacies and hospitals, such as large spikes in orders or unusual increases in dosages prescribed. Eyre provides ample evidence that the largest drug distributors intentionally ignored this responsibility, in part to save themselves the effort, but, more important, to maximize their sales. Civil lawsuits in New York, Vermont, and Washington accused these distributors of intentionally devising systems to evade regulators. Specifically, the suits claimed that the distributors warned pharmacies at risk of being reported to the Drug Enforcement Administration, helped pharmacies circumvent limits on how many opioids they were allowed to buy, and provided advance notice to pharmacies on the rare occasions that the distributors were pushed to audit the prescriptions from the pharmacy. Rather than acknowledging that extraordinarily large or frequent orders were suspicious (a term that would require reporting under federal law), employees and executives of the distributors would describe these transactions as unusual.[16] As the epidemic developed, the distributors continued these illegal actions to maximize their own profits.

Eyre began researching the distributors when someone tipped off the newspaper he worked for, the *Charleston Gazette-Mail*, that Denise Morrisey, the wife of West Virginia attorney general Patrick Morrisey, worked as a political lobbyist for drug distributor Cardinal Health. Patrick Morrisey inherited a lawsuit from his predecessor that accused Cardinal Health of illegal and inappropriate distribution of opioids. Eyre provides substantial evidence that Morrisey hampered the lawsuit being prosecuted out of his office, even as Cardinal Health made hefty

contributions to his political campaigns. Morrisey claimed he recused himself from involvement in the case due to the conflict of interest. But as Eyre documents, Morrisey continued to direct his staff's handling of the case, met personally with Cardinal Health lawyers and executives (as well as representatives from McKesson), hired a Cardinal Health lawyer to head his campaign transition team, and threatened the *Gazette-Mail* for covering the story. When Eyre asked Cardinal Health why it was funding Morrisey's inaugural party while his office was suing the company, he received no answer. But Morrisey did react to the question: he sent Eyre an email demanding to meet with his editors and publisher, accused the reporter of malice, falsely claimed that his wife had nothing to do with Cardinal Health's distribution in West Virginia, and ordered Eyre not to publish anything else on the topic until after Morrisey met with the publisher.

By 2020, the three leading prescription opioid distributors had agreed to pay $21 billion to state and local governments to end thousands of lawsuits over the companies' role in the opioid epidemic. In a separate set of legal actions, in December 2020, the Department of Justice (DOJ) accused Walmart of fueling the opioid crisis by ignoring obvious signals that, in violation of federal regulations, its pharmacists weren't properly screening painkiller prescriptions. In its civil suit, DOJ lawyers contended that Walmart executives set up a system that turned its 5,000 in-store pharmacies into one of the country's biggest suppliers of highly addictive opioid painkillers. The chain allegedly used low prices to lure customers and then demanded that pharmacists pick up the pace of filling prescriptions, leaving little time for proper monitoring. Walmart collected data on physicians it labeled "problem prescribers" but didn't share the data with its pharmacists or federal regulators. Walmart's leadership also

stood accused of ignoring staff members' warnings about suspicious patterns of prescriptions. States, cities, and counties have also filed more than 2,000 lawsuits accusing Walmart of intentionally ignoring suspicious prescriptions for painkillers in order to profit from opioid addictions. In the first trial against national pharmacy chains to go to court, a federal jury found Walmart, CVS, and Walgreens guilty in November 2021 of contributing to opioid overdoses and deaths in two Ohio counties by ignoring red flags about suspicious drug orders both in their stores and at their corporate headquarters. A judge was scheduled to determine how much each company should pay the counties in the months ahead.[17]

Nothing about the allegedly criminal behavior of the physicians, pharmacies, and distributors (not to mention the corrupt or incompetent behavior of local, state, and federal officials) that I've described lets Purdue Pharma off the hook for the opioid crisis. But the actions of these complicitors highlights that it is a mistake to blame only the primary wrongdoer for a crisis or scandal. In every crisis described in this book, a very visible individual or company was primarily responsible for carrying out the bad behavior. And in every crisis, other actors had incentives to help the core harm doer meet their goal. In the case of opioids, that goal was to maximize profits by contributing to the spread of an epidemic. Across all of these stories, the core actor depended on the active collaboration of true partners to do harm. Unfortunately, complicity was easy for them to obtain.

True Partners in the Holocaust

In 1933, the European Jewish population stood at about nine million people. Most Jews lived in Germany or in countries that

Nazi Germany would occupy or control during World War II. Between 1941 and 1945, the Nazis and their complicitors carried out the Holocaust, the systematic, state-sponsored murder of two-thirds of all European Jews—about six million people. The Nazis claimed that Germans were genetically superior to Jews, whom they considered to be a threat to the German "race." The Nazis also targeted the Roma (sometimes derogatorily called "gypsies" in English), Poles, Russians, the disabled, and homosexuals. For political reasons, they also went after communists, socialists, and Jehovah's Witnesses. The murders were ordered by Adolf Hitler and Heinrich Himmler, the two most powerful Nazi leaders. But killing many millions of people required the help of partners.

The Nazis received help across Europe. Austria, where Hitler was born, provided one-third of the personnel for the Nazis' paramilitary extermination units and commanded four of the six main concentration camps where the Jews were gassed.[18] With their long histories of antisemitism, Ukraine and the Baltic states were receptive to Nazi ideology and intimidated by German military power, and participated in the mass killings. But the government that may be most closely associated with "collaboration" with the Nazis was the Vichy government of France.

The Vichy regime was established on July 10, 1940, after Germany's invasion of France. After the French government surrendered, the Nazis divided France into an occupied zone, which covered the north and west of the country, and a "free zone" in the south. Marshal Philippe Pétain, a French World War I hero, was put in charge of the southern part of France, or what became known as the Vichy government because its headquarters were in the town of Vichy. Pétain and his associates viewed Germany's conquest of France as an opportunity

to wipe out the left-wing values that dominated France in the 1930s. Pétain dispensed with parliamentary democracy and worked with Nazi Germany, presenting it as a new beginning for France.

The Vichy government was quick to enact its own anti-semitic laws while also repealing French laws against stigmatizing groups of people based on their race or religion. The Vichy government seized Jewish businesses and prevented Jews from being employed in the army and the public sector. In 1942, Vichy police rounded up 76,000 Jews for deportation to concentration camps. Coordinating with the Nazis, the Vichy government transferred thousands of French workers to German-controlled ports to work for the Nazis. Some ship workers objected, but most were willing and effective workers for the Nazis.

For forty years after World War II ended in 1945, the French government denied its role in the evil instigated by the Nazis. French war hero Charles de Gaulle led the Free French resistance against the Vichy regime but falsely claimed at the end of the war that "only a handful of scoundrels" had behaved badly during the French occupation.[19] Denial, he argued, was the best way to preserve national unity. François Mitterrand, France's president from 1981 to 1995, also refused to apologize for his country's behavior: because Vichy had broken with France, he argued, the republic bore no responsibility. Finally, in 1995, President Jacques Chirac apologized on behalf of the French Republic for its complicity in the Holocaust.

Hitler was clearly the prototype of evil, but he could only accomplish his destruction with the complicity of many others. He needed the complicity of his fellow Germans, many of whom were willing to carry out his orders. He also needed complicity from businesses inside and outside of Germany to

produce the war machinery, often with Jewish slave labor. He needed the complicity of antisemitic partners in the countries that Germany invaded. And he even benefited from antisemitic views expressed by prominent figures in the United States, such as Charles Lindbergh and the America First Committee, influences that delayed the U.S. government's recognition of the Holocaust and its entry into the war.

To take one example, antisemites were influential in the U.S. response to the *Motorschiff St. Louis*, a German ocean liner that carried 937 Jews fleeing Nazi Germany in 1939.[20] The Jews planned to emigrate to Cuba and believed they had proper landing permits. But antisemitic influences in Cuba succeeded in invalidating their paperwork. When Cuba refused to let the boat land, it headed to the United States and Canada. Both nations refused to save what came to be known as "The Voyage of the Damned." While the U.S. government, under President Franklin D. Roosevelt, did try to get the Jews admitted to Cuba and eventually negotiated to arrange their admission to a combination of the United Kingdom, Belgium, the Netherlands, and France, antisemitism kept the United States itself from admitting the refugees. The U.S. government rigidly stuck with a quota system that capped the number of Germans and Austrians entering the country. Many of these passengers were later caught by the Nazis and killed in concentration camps. Roosevelt had considered enacting legislation to do more to rescue Jewish refugees but dropped the idea, understanding that it would be politically unpopular.

Complicity with Trump: The Early Years

Donald Trump's campaign slogans, "America First" and "Make America Great Again," were emotional appeals that conveyed

nostalgia for a time when white privilege went unchecked. Trump himself is a poster boy for white privilege: he was raised wealthy, gained admission to the prestigious Wharton School with help from his father, cheated his way into a draft deferment during the Vietnam War, and embarked on his failed business career with a substantial loan from his father that he never repaid.[21] Throughout his life, Trump made racist business decisions and backed cruel, discriminatory policies that favored whites, even as he denied that these policies and decisions were racially motivated.[22] His core motivating values were apparent in 1973, when the Department of Justice sued Trump and his father for refusing to rent apartments in their thirty-nine New York buildings to African Americans, Puerto Ricans, and other minorities.[23] In 1975, Trump Management Company settled the suit, agreeing to pay undisclosed penalties and to report vacancies in its apartments to authorities, among other terms.

Trump's rise within Republican circles grew out of his promotion of "birtherism"—a false and racist conspiracy theory that Barack Obama was not an American citizen. "I have people that have been studying [Obama's birth certificate] and they cannot believe what they're finding," Trump said in 2011. "If he wasn't born in this country, which is a real possibility . . . then he has pulled one of the great cons in the history of politics."[24] Trump also repeated false claims that Obama was Muslim. As would become a pattern, Trump produced no evidence for his claims, despite asserting that they were based on objective evidence.

By integrating extreme views of Blacks, immigrants, and Muslims, birtherism combined three prejudices into one false conspiracy theory, writes Adam Serwer in the *Atlantic*. Attracting white voters who were unable to accept the idea of a Black president, birtherism helped launch Trump's

presidential campaign views. "The insistence that it was a fringe belief undersells the fact that [birtherism] was one of the most important political developments of the past decade," writes Serwer.[25] Trump had found his base.

Many in the Republican mainstream snubbed Trump during the campaign, questioning his intelligence, knowledge, and integrity. But Trump's views during his first presidential race were enthusiastically endorsed by the racist, nationalist right wing of the Republican Party. "A Trump Administration is a return to the America that won the West, landed on the moon, and built an economy and military that stunned the world," wrote the white supremacist journal *American Renaissance* in 2016.[26]

Trump's closest ideological partner in his campaign at the beginning of his presidency was Steve Bannon, the executive chairman of Breitbart News, an alt-right platform that enthusiastically promoted views rooted in white supremacism, authoritarianism, racism, sexism, and antisemitism. Under Bannon, Breitbart headlines included the following:

- "Bill Kristol: Republican Spoiler, Renegade Jew"
- "There's No Bias against Women in Tech, They Just Suck at Interviews"
- "Planned Parenthood's Body Count under Cecile Richards Is Up to Half a Holocaust"
- "Racist, Pro-Nazi Roots of Planned Parenthood Revealed"[27]

Because of his work at Breitbart, Bannon was a hero to white supremacists, including antisemites, neo-Nazis, and the Ku Klux Klan. After Trump appointed him campaign manager, three months before the 2016 election, Bannon developed Trump's most divisive and racist campaign promises, including

his vow to ban Muslim immigrants from the United States and a nationwide stop-and-frisk policy that would allow Black and Latino men to be targeted for interrogation even with little evidence of a crime.

Upon taking office, Trump appointed Bannon to the role of chief strategist. Bannon collaborated with White House adviser Stephen Miller on the chaotic Muslim ban. Bannon was also behind Trump's assertion that "very fine people on both sides" were involved in the white supremacist "Unite the Right" rally in Charlottesville, Virginia, in August 2017—remarks widely criticized for implying moral equivalence between the white supremacist marchers and those who protested against them. Frequently characterized by observers as Trump's political Svengali, Bannon was an expert at convincing people to believe fake news, a strategy that proved central to Trump's presidency.[28] Eventually, Bannon's influence faded following a number of controversies, including Trump's decision to appoint him to the National Security Council.

Those who were in lockstep with Donald Trump's core identity—who backed him in the 2016 Republican primary and were thrilled when he won the party's nomination—were his central complicitors, the true partners in his wrongdoing.

Why Do True Partners Help Harm Doers?

As we'll see in the chapters and profiles that follow, the psychology behind why complicitors choose to go along with wrongdoing is often complex. The true partners that I've described in this chapter have simpler motives: they align closely with the core goals of the wrongdoer. Whether it is selling more opioids and earning more profit, eliminating the "Jewish problem," or advancing the interests of white Americans, true partners

succeed if the core wrongdoer succeeds. In the language of economics, the interests of the wrongdoer and the complicitor are aligned. If the wrongdoer succeeds, the complicitor gains money, influence, power, or their preferred policies.

Of course, the goals of the wrongdoer and their complicitors don't always overlap perfectly. I use the term "true partner" to refer to a very strong overlap between the core goals of the harm doer and complicitors. In the WeWork case that we pick up in the next chapter, the interests of Rebekah Neumann, the spouse of WeWork founder and CEO Adam Neumann, heavily overlapped with his interests. After they destroyed billions of dollars in value for their investors and employees, the Neumanns walked away with over a billion dollars and moved to another country (Israel) to avoid the scorn and recrimination of those they had harmed. But, as we'll see, other partners collaborated with Adam Neumann extensively without being fully aligned with his goals.

3

Collaborators

In 2017, I visited the Manhattan office that a consulting client of mine was renting from WeWork, the heavily funded start-up that claimed it was revolutionizing the concept of coworking spaces. I was impressed by the design of the space, my client's ability to rent a small amount of space in a great part of the city without making a long-term commitment, and the excellent beverages that were thrown in. I was also surprised by how little they were paying for the space—not something you commonly hear about commercial rents in New York. And I appreciated the efficiency of creating a low-transaction-cost opportunity for start-ups to rent just the space they needed, which seemed to reduce waste.

Of course, WeWork didn't invent the concept of coworking. In fact, WeWork tended to open locations within blocks of competing workspace companies. But WeWork had something that the competition lacked: Adam Neumann. Tall, with flowing black hair and a penchant for spouting lofty ideas, Neumann was a charismatic figure who presented WeWork not as an office rental company but as a communal tech firm that would

bring people together and change the way they worked. The rise and fall of WeWork is well documented in Charles Duhigg's 2020 *New Yorker* article, Reeves Weideman's book *Billion Dollar Loser*, and Eliot Brown and Maureen Farrell's book *The Cult of We*.[1]

"Our company is about *we* and about *collaboration*," Neumann said at a coworking-industry conference in 2012, when the company was just getting started. "Together, we can build a community that can change the world."[2] WeWork's amenities and hip vibe were central to its image, along with the sense of spirituality and community it ingrained in its employees. Neumann touted the potential for its "members," or renters, to interact with others in their coworking space, potentially creating new and lucrative business opportunities.[3] WeWork's networking technology was supposed to facilitate the growth of members' businesses. But the actual technology available (that is, Wi-Fi connections) in WeWork locations was often poor, and most WeWork members didn't actually value the alleged networking opportunities. Most simply wanted a cheap workspace with free lattes thrown in.[4]

Like many tech firms, WeWork sought to create a near-monopoly in its space so that it might eventually command enormous long-term profit margins. To meet this goal, WeWork focused on securing huge investments from venture capital firms, which allowed it to clobber the competition on price. More centered on growth and image development than short term profit, WeWork offered low rents that led to mounting operating losses and put competitors, such as NextSpace Coworking, out of business. This business model, which made WeWork dependent on an ever-increasing influx in investment dollars to cover its operating losses, was never sustainable, as investors should have recognized. Neumann's knack for

amassing billions of dollars in VC funds despite having no viable business model was one of the greatest scams of the 2010s.

We tend to view collaboration—the act of coordinating with others in the pursuit of shared interests—in a positive light. When we collaborate with others, we have both shared and differing interests. For example, on a project team, you and your team members might want to collectively find a solution to a problem but disagree about the preferred solution, who will get the credit, and so on. Similarly, investors in a company typically collaborate with its founders in aiming for financial success, but their interests are rarely perfectly aligned. Through negotiation and cooperation, parties can dovetail their interests and each get more of what they want.

But as we'll see with the story of WeWork, collaboration isn't always beneficial, even if it temporarily improves the lot of everyone at the negotiating table. When we collaborate with people who act in egregious ways, we are complicit in their harm. When we form agreements that benefit us and a harm doer at the expense of people who are not at the table, we destroy societal value.

In his article about WeWork, Duhigg describes the complicity of venture capitalists in Neumann's scam. These investors weren't inspired by Neumann's spiritual vision but rather by their belief that WeWork could become the dominant player in the space-sharing economy. They just needed Neumann to maintain WeWork's pizzazz until the company could go public, at which point they could sell their shares for a large profit. What might happen next to WeWork employees and customers was of far less concern to the venture capitalists.

Bruce Dunlevie of Silicon Valley firm Benchmark Capital, an early funder of eBay, Twitter, and Instagram, joined WeWork's board of directors and was an early and enthusiastic

champion of Neumann. In 2012, Dunlevie persuaded Benchmark to become WeWork's first major investor, with a $15 million investment as part of a $17 million fundraising round. The investment put WeWork's valuation at $97 million. Dunlevie admitted to a skeptical partner at Benchmark that he didn't see how WeWork could turn a profit, but he was dazzled by Neumann: "Let's give him some money," Dunlevie said, "and he'll figure it out."[5]

By the end of 2014, WeWork's investors included JPMorgan Chase, T. Rowe Price, Wellington Management, Goldman Sachs Group, Mort Zuckerman, and, unfortunately, the Harvard Corporation—the governing board that manages the endowment of the university I work for. WeWork had raised over half a billion dollars from venture capitalists, and JPMorgan Chase CEO Jamie Dimon began advising Neumann on WeWork's growth. In addition to its investments and advisory services, JPMorgan Chase also provided huge loans to WeWork and personal loans to the Neumanns totaling about $95 million, including mortgages for five mansions. The bank was clearly courting Neumann in the hope of being appointed the underwriter of WeWork's highly anticipated initial public offering (IPO). Underwriting a highly valued IPO can be an enormous source of profit for investment banks.

Armed with these huge investments, WeWork was growing fast, with plans to open sixty locations in twelve cities. Yet the company was losing $6 million a month.[6] The Neumanns were bleeding resources from WeWork at the expense of employees and the company. For example, using loans from the banks that were courting them, the Neumanns bought buildings and then leased them to WeWork at prices favorable to themselves—an egregious case of self-dealing. To impress investors like Dunlevie and Dimon, WeWork became skilled at temporarily turning

rental locations in New York into communal, high-tech work-spaces. The last-minute staging was part of Neumann's scam.

By the end of 2016, without doing basic due diligence, investors had poured another billion dollars into WeWork, allowing Neumann to pump food and water into an inert business model. As operating losses spiraled, the firm needed new and more investment funds to avoid being felled by its operating losses, in the manner of a Ponzi scheme. Neumann clearly had a knack for convincing seemingly sophisticated investors to invest in his shallow and deceitful vision. And the person who would become the biggest complicitor in venture capital history was waiting in the wings.

Masayoshi ("Masa") Son, the famed SoftBank venture capitalist, had a history of both enormous investment hits and misses. Thanks to his early investment in Alibaba, he was at one point the richest person on the planet. In 2017, SoftBank raised $100 billion to start the Vision Fund, a venture capital fund four times larger than any previous fund. Mohammed bin Salman, the crown prince of Saudi Arabia, invested $45 billion in the Vision Fund as part of his efforts to expand Saudi Arabian influence beyond oil. Bin Salman would become notorious for his association with the planning of the October 2018 murder of Jamal Khashoggi, a Saudi journalist and critic of the crown prince. Additional billions came to Son's fund from the Abu Dhabi government.

Neumann managed to score a meeting with Son. In December 2016, Son visited president-elect Donald Trump at Trump Tower and had a two-hour visit scheduled with Neumann at WeWork after that.[7] But the visit with Trump ran late, and Son only had twelve minutes to spend at WeWork. As he departed, he asked Neumann to join him in his car. Neumann prepared to present his investor deck, but Son told him to put the slides

away. The good news for Neumann was that Son trusted his intuition over the careful analysis that his colleagues at Soft-Bank might have recommended. Knowing that he was about to have $100 billion to invest, Son was eager to find promising business opportunities. Son pulled out his iPad and sketched out a deal to invest $4.4 billion in WeWork, with a valuation of the company slightly above $20 billion.

When the Vision Fund investment went through, early investors—but few WeWork employees—had the opportunity to sell their shares in WeWork. Of SoftBank's $4.4 billion invest ment, $1.3 billion was used to buy back shares. Early WeWork investor Benchmark, appearing to identify the gaping holes in the company's business model, sold as many shares as was allowed—$129 million. The Neumanns took $361 million out of the company.

Thanks to Son, Neumann was able to extend his unsustain-able adventure. The cash infusion gave Neumann plenty of funds for growth—as well as a complicitor who would fuel his worst instincts. At WeWork, Neumann had already created a work culture that embraced cocaine, alcohol, and spirituality rather than financial responsibility. Son pushed Neumann fur-ther away from rationality. "In a fight, who wins—the smart guy or the crazy guy?" he asked after Neumann flew to Tokyo to celebrate the deal.

"Crazy guy," said Neumann.

"You are correct," Son said. "But you . . . are not crazy *enough*."[8]

With Son's encouragement and funding, WeWork ventured beyond the office-space business. Neumann started WeGrow, a private school in Manhattan's tony Chelsea neighborhood; Rise by We, a luxury gym; and WeLive, a proposed extension of WeWork into housing, with shared living spaces and services, such as laundry, cleaning, and cooking, and, once again, a cool

vibe. WeWork also made twenty acquisitions between 2015 and 2019, many of them connected to Neumann's personal interests rather than to WeWork's core business. These included a $13 million investment in a company that made artificial-wave pools—Neumann was obsessed with surfing. With these moves into other domains, WeWork continued its focus on growth at the expense of profitability and sustainability. The company's name changed to WeCompany to highlight its breadth. Neumann trademarked the word "We"—and then sold it back to his own company for $5.9 million in stock.

As Neumann's unfocused acquisitions, greed, and deception grew, WeWork's investors stood back and did little to intervene. Happy to profit from Son's investment, Benchmark was eager to earn more. With each new private investment, the implied valuation of Benchmark's remaining shares in WeWork skyrocketed. But by 2018, WeWork was again running out of cash, with losses projected at almost $2 billion for the year.[9] Son and Neumann were working on a new, even more massive infusion of cash from the Vision Fund, rumored to be as high as $20 billion, which could be used to buy out existing WeWork shareholders, including Benchmark and WeWork employees, and keep WeWork private for a significant period of time. But while Son bonded with Neumann, many key executives at SoftBank were increasingly skeptical of his investments in WeWork. Near the end of 2018, the governments of Saudi Arabia and Abu Dhabi exercised their veto rights on Vision Fund investments, which prevented Son from closing the new deal with WeWork.[10] Their decision to exercise their veto rights was key to changing the course of the history of WeWork.

After the Vision Fund investment evaporated, WeWork was desperate for cash. Drawing on money from outside of Vision

Fund, Son invested another $1 billion on January 8, 2019. Son and Neumann agreed to set WeWork's valuation at $47 billion.[11] They had the power to set the valuation as long as Son was willing to only take one forty-seventh of the firm for the new billion-dollar investment. The private nature of the transaction allowed them to keep details of WeWork's operations and finances private, but they did benefit from the media reporting that WeWork was now worth $47 billion.

Having secured "only" an extra billion, WeWork would soon need significant additional funding to stay afloat. This led Neumann to launch an IPO process. Selling stock shares to the public could raise significant amounts of money.

To court Neumann's business, investment banks continued to allow him to delude himself about WeWork's value. Just as you might not hire a real estate agent who tells you that your house is worth less than you think it is, banks are unlikely to win an IPO underwriting assignment if they suggest a valuation that the potential client thinks is too low. Predictably, banks provided huge valuations of WeWork for its IPO. Morgan Stanley advised setting WeWork's valuation at $104 billion, while Goldman Sachs recommended a price closer to $96 billion.[12] Neglecting their responsibilities to other shareholders, WeWork's board of directors, including Dunlevie and other early investors, were also complicit: they kept quiet about Neumann's destructive behavior and hoped the IPO would go through so that investors could sell their shares.

Because venture capital firms are most commonly private, limited disclosure of their financial data is required of them. As we've seen, many of their investment decisions are made based on reputation and intuition rather than appropriate due diligence. The IPO process for private firms is different. If a firm wants to go public, the Securities and Exchange Commission (SEC) requires

it to file a so-called S-1 form, which first needs to be approved by the company's board. The S-1 requires a great deal of specific, well-defined financial information. Rather than coughing up such data, Adam and Rebekah Neumann approached WeWork's S-1 like a school art project. They wrote about WeWork's spiritual mission "to elevate the world's consciousness," invented their own financial metrics, and flooded the document with lush photographs. The document raised eyebrows, but WeWork employees, board members, lawyers, accountants, consultants, and investment bankers all signed off on it. "Basically, we chose willful ignorance and greed over admitting this was obviously batshit crazy," one former WeWork executive told Duhigg.[13] Everyone just wanted to get to the finish line.

While the Neumanns were proud of their S-1, and those who stood to profit went along with it, potential investors were frightened by how much conventional information about finances and business practices was missing from the form. They pointed out the obvious: WeWork's business model simply didn't make sense.

The investment banks leading the IPO found that no one was buying. They lowered WeWork's proposed valuation multiple times but never enough to attract significant numbers of investors. By August 2019, the valuation target had been dropped from the early estimates of around $47 to $100 billion to between $20 and $30 billion. Still no interest. By September, WeWork's proposed valuation was lowered to $10 billion. Still no one bit. On September 16, WeWork canceled the IPO, and Dunlevie pressured Neumann to step down, which he did.

By October, WeWork was running out of cash. JPMorgan and SoftBank each offered to buy out the company. WeWork's board accepted SoftBank's offer of about $8 billion for the whole firm, far less than the $12.8 billion that investors had

provided to WeWork. By May 2020, as the COVID-19 crisis hit and WeWork renters started working from home, SoftBank valued WeWork at $2.9 billion.

When we think of venture capitalists and bankers weighing investments, we often think of MBA types engaging in complex financial analysis and thorough due diligence aimed at determining the long-term sustainability of a business. We think of rationality rather than gullibility, skepticism rather than a willingness to be charmed by a charlatan. These impressions of the investment community are contradicted by the WeWork story, where intuition, wild claims, and a fast-talking CEO prevailed. Unlike the true partners described in chapter 2, WeWork's complicitors may not have shared the harm doer's core values. And when they had enough information to know the problems with Adam Neumann's presentation of the firm's financials, they failed to alert other investors. Their negligence created an environment where most WeWork employees were never able to benefit from cashing in stock options, many investors suffered massive losses, and competitors were unfairly driven out of business by WeWork pricing its product well below cost.

The Complicity of Unions and Government in Dieselgate

In 1934, Adolf Hitler commissioned Ferdinand Porsche, founder of the Porsche automotive company, to build a *volkswagen*, or "car for the people"—a car that any German family could afford. During World War II, the company Porsche founded to meet that goal, Volkswagen (VW), was converted to produce military vehicles, which were built with slave labor. An estimated 15,000 Jews from the Arbeitsdorf concentration camp worked at Volkswagen during the war, and many died from abuse.[14]

VW's authoritarian leadership survived into the twenty-first century. In 2007, the company developed a plan to become the world's largest manufacturer of passenger cars; chairman Ferdinand Piëch and CEO Martin Winterkorn set a sales target of ten million cars a year, well above the six million produced in 2007. Central to this goal was the development and marketing of a "clean diesel" engine, a feature of enormous value to the environmentally focused U.S. market. VW developed a diesel engine that it claimed was environmentally friendly. The car was a hit in the States. How did VW do it? Instead of producing engines that were environmentally friendly, the company developed computer codes that instructed its cars to cheat on emissions tests. Once uncovered, the cheating scandal came to be known as Dieselgate. "This is a case of deliberate, massive fraud perpetrated by VW management," concluded Judge Sean F. Cox in a U.S. Federal District Court as he imposed a $2.8 billion fine on the company.[15]

Experts estimate that excess pollution created by VW's diesel cars between 2008 and 2015 was responsible for the loss of 45,000 disability-adjusted life years (DALYs).[16] DALY is a technical term used to measure years of healthy life lost to disease, disability, and premature death; one DALY refers to the loss of one year of full health. By 2015, Winterkorn had resigned in disgrace, and Oliver Schmidt, VW's emissions compliance manager in the United States, was in prison. As of June 2020, the scandal had cost VW $33.3 billion in fines, penalties, financial settlements, and buyback costs. Senior leadership tried to blame a small number of mid-level engineers for Dieselgate, but that notion is inconsistent with how engineers build complex control systems and with how VW was run. Indeed, significant evidence emerged of a broad conspiracy within the organization. One Volkswagen employee, Daniel Donovan, filed a whistleblower lawsuit in Michigan that provided evidence that

coworkers illegally deleted electronic data shortly after the U.S. government accused VW of cheating on emissions tests. Donovan asserts he was fired because his superiors believed he was about to report the company to U.S. authorities.

Unions and government regulators were also complicit in the Dieselgate story. In 1937, the Nazis took control of the Volkswagen project and effectively eliminated the employee union and confiscated its wealth. After World War II, to keep labor from claiming compensation for the 1937 theft, worker representatives at VW received enormous influence over the company's future; they currently hold ten of the twenty seats on its board. Two government representatives of Lower Saxony, the state where VW is located, typically side with the workers. The Porsche and Piëch families hold another five seats.

The unions and the government of Lower Saxony received job security for the employees they represented in return for their complicity. As long as VW guaranteed jobs, the unions and the Lower Saxony government condoned unethical and even illegal behavior by VW's leadership. "There's no other company where the owners and the unions are working so closely together as Volkswagen," a former VW senior executive told the *New York Times*. "What management, the government, and the unions all want is full employment, and the more jobs, the better. . . . They'll look the other way about anything."[17] To keep union leaders happy, VW executives offered them business trips, which included prostitutes, shopping, and Viagra.[18] In 2005, Klaus Volkert, then the lead worker representative at VW, was found guilty of accepting a two-million-euro bribe from Peter Hartz, a VW management board member.

Beyond Dieselgate, intentionally lax regulation contributed to interconnected emissions cheating scandals in Germany.

From 2006 to 2014, the "circle of five" German automotive companies—VW, Daimler, BMW, Audi, and Porsche (the latter two being owned by VW), along with Bosch and other parts providers—were found guilty of conspiring to equip their vehicles with inferior emissions equipment, causing thousands of deaths annually by emitting harmful chemicals into the air.[19] Without the complicity of the unions and government, it is unlikely that VW could have destroyed as many lives as it did. The unions and government did not share in the profits from selling more VW automobiles, but they were interested in the jobs and political benefits that came with them.

Mitch and Lindsey

Before Donald Trump received the Republican nomination for president in 2016, Republican South Carolina senator Lindsey Graham called him a "jackass," a "nutjob," "crazy," "not fit to be president," and a "race-baiting, xenophobic, religious bigot." He said that the Republican Party had gone "batshit crazy" to nominate Trump. In March 2016, he tweeted, "You know how to make America great? . . . Tell Trump to go to hell."[20]

Senate majority leader Mitch McConnell, a Republican from Kentucky, generally expresses himself more cautiously than Graham. But in reaction to Trump's nomination, he suggested that the candidate needed to select a running mate with care, given his own lack of experience, and added that Trump didn't understand "the issues."[21] After the *Access Hollywood* tape in which Trump boasted about assaulting women was released, McConnell described the comments as "repugnant and unacceptable in any circumstance" and called for Trump to "apologize directly to women and girls everywhere."[22]

During the 2016 campaign, many other Republicans expressed concerns about Trump. But once Trump was elected, most Republicans became complicit in his worst behaviors.

Graham, for example, repeatedly made excuses for Trump's abuses of power.[23] The senator had been part of a bipartisan effort to draft comprehensive immigration reform in 2014, and when Trump was running for president, Graham called his proposed border wall with Mexico "stupid and illegal."[24] But after Trump's election, Graham enthusiastically supported Trump's immigration plan, including the border wall. As a member of the Senate Judiciary Committee, the senator also threw his support behind Trump's judicial nominees.

Similarly, once Trump took office, McConnell's criticisms of him came to a halt. During the Trump administration, the Senate leader focused primarily on getting as many conservative judges approved by Congress as possible. Writing in the *New York Times*, Jennifer Senior chalks up McConnell's tolerance of Trump to his willingness to make whatever trade is necessary to get what he wants: "If hitching his wagon to a sub-literate mob boss with a fondness for white supremacists and a penchant for conspiracy theories and a sociopath's smirking disregard for the truth meant getting those tax cuts and those conservative judges . . . hey, that's the cost of doing business."[25]

Graham and McConnell were never true partners with Trump, the way that Steve Bannon was. They didn't share Trump's open disdain for democracy and the rule of law, or his support for white supremacists. Rather, they were traders, willing to work with a harm doer to get what they wanted. McConnell made "a Faustian deal for all those judges," according to Congressman John Yarmouth, a Democrat from Kentucky.[26] McConnell was central to installing more than two hundred conservative federal judges, including three Supreme Court

justices. Similarly, Graham downplayed evidence that Trump attempted to blackmail the Ukrainian president Volodymyr Zelenskyy into launching a phony, politically motivated investigation into Biden's son Hunter.

As historian Anne Applebaum presciently observed in June 2020,

> The price of collaboration in America has already turned out to be extraordinarily high. And yet, the movement down the slippery slope continues, just as it did in so many occupied countries in the past. First Trump's enablers accepted lies about the inauguration; now they accept terrible tragedy and the loss of American leadership in the world. Worse could follow. Come November, will they tolerate—even abet—an assault on the electoral system: open efforts to prevent postal voting, to shut polling stations, to scare people away from voting? Will they countenance violence, as the president's social-media fans incite demonstrators to launch physical attacks on state and city officials?[27]

As we know, they did. After Trump lost, Graham backed his lies about rampant voter fraud and supported his efforts to overturn the election results. Graham and McConnell refused to acknowledge Biden's victory until December 15, the day after the Electoral College certified the election results. When Congress convened to count the Electoral College vote on January 6, McConnell finally refuted Trump's attempts to overturn the election, saying, "If this election were overturned by mere allegations from the losing side, our democracy would enter a death spiral."[28] After the attack on the Capitol that day, the Senate leader reportedly held Trump directly responsible and favored impeaching him, yet he refused to convene the Senate for an impeachment trial before Trump left office.[29] When the

Senate finally tried Trump in February, after Biden had taken office, McConnell voted to acquit based on a technicality: the fact that Trump was no longer in office—though it had been his decision not to hold a trial while Trump was president.

Authoritarian leaders with racist tendencies are emerging in many parts of the world. Holding their supporting cast accountable for their complicity may be the key to stopping them.

Why They Do It

Like the true partners we saw in chapter 2, collaborators focus on how they would benefit from the wrongdoer's behavior. True partners share core values with the harm doer, while collaborators are willing to work with the harm doer as long as they get what they want in return. In the process, they are often willing to escalate their commitment to the harm doer and justify their willingness to help that person engage in unethical action.

Yet collaborators' ties to their harm doer are inherently unstable because these coalitions are created as a matter of convenience. Some collaborators, such as Graham and McConnell, fully escalate their commitment even when the harm doer has crossed the collaborators' ethical red lines, as Applebaum correctly predicted. But others stick around only as long as they're getting what they need from the coalition. As Trump's national security adviser, General H. R. McMaster was viewed as steady, intellectual, and competent. He quit in 2018 after repeatedly clashing with Trump and disapproving of the incompetence the president displayed in negotiations with Iran, North Korea, and Russia. Rex Tillerson quit as secretary of state in 2018 after realizing that Trump was a "moron."[30] Gary Cohn left his position as director of the National Economic Council after Trump said

there had been "very fine people on both sides" at the deadly white supremacist rally in Charlottesville, Virginia.[31] General James Mattis reached his breaking point when the president abruptly abandoned the Kurds, America's longtime allies in the war against the Islamic State. All presidential administrations experience turnover, but the 92 percent turnover of the Trump administration was extreme.[32] A key reason for it, in addition to Trump's volatility, immorality, and incompetence, was that many members of his administration were never his true partners. As collaborators who decided to try to look beyond Trump's many flaws to further their goals, they didn't hesitate to leave when they didn't like the deal anymore. Unfortunately, most of them had already helped Trump commit enormous harm.

Much of my career has focused on negotiation. I have written a couple of books on negotiation, conducted dozens of experimental studies exploring how people think when negotiating, and taught tens of thousands of MBA and executive students how to negotiate more effectively. The negotiation literature is filled with stories of parties collaborating so that each side can get what they want. When collaborators make trades across issues, negotiation scholars call it "logrolling."[33] Logrolling involves parties making concessions on issues of importance to their counterpart in return for concessions on issues they themselves value more. In politics, logrolling often refers to combining multiple issues into one bill so that all members of a coalition get what's most important to them. In the U.S. government, logrolling dates back to at least 1790, when Representative James Madison and Thomas Jefferson, then George Washington's secretary of state, reached an agreement with U.S. Treasury secretary Alexander Hamilton over two issues. In their "Compromise of 1790," as fans of the musical *Hamilton* will recall, Jefferson and Madison agreed

to Hamilton's preference to have the federal government pay states' Revolutionary War debts in return for Hamilton agreeing to Jefferson and Madison's preference to put the nation's capital in the South.

Generally, negotiation experts present logrolling as a positive behavior used by wise negotiators—a way to efficiently integrate the interests of both parties in a deal. But what about instances where the parties are creating value by taking it from others? James Gillespie and I coined the term "parasitic integration" to describe agreements where negotiators create value by taking it from parties who aren't at the bargaining table.[34] For example, two companies in the same industry that reach a secret, illegal deal to keep prices high might be creating value for themselves, but they are also engaging in collusion that harms the public. Similarly, when collaborators support Trump's initiatives for authoritarian rule and white supremacy, in return for Trump enacting very favorable tax rates for the rich and appointing right-leaning judges to the courts, the losses to those being harmed from the deal can be massive, and those who are complicit should be held responsible. From an ethical perspective, the goodness of a collaboration must be assessed based on the overall positive or negative value it creates for or imposes on society, rather than merely on how it affects the collaborators.[35]

When a negotiator gives an evasive and potentially misleading answer to a question, without lying outright, is that unethical? People have differing views of what constitutes unethical behavior in negotiation. What is clear, however, is that how we interpret the questionable behavior is affected by who engaged in the questionable practice. We tend to justify the behavior when we are the culprit but judge our negotiating counterparts far more harshly for the same behavior, for instance. We

also tend to excuse members of our "tribe," including other members of our organization, division, family, religion, race, or nationality.[36] We also tend to be collaborators with others in our tribe, as was the case for many affiliated with WeWork and Volkswagen as well as the Republicans surrounding Trump. Thus, we tend to overlook the questionable behavior of collaborators in our group. This allows us to continue to work with people whose behavior we would otherwise condemn, absent this bias.

On the flip side, tribes often have enemies, and we interpret our enemies' behavior more harshly than the behavior of people we do not even know.[37] As a result, when we see a football player on "our" team hit by a football player on the opposing team, we view the opponent's behavior as more unethical than when we support neither team.[38] We also use the behavior of our enemies to justify questionable behavior on our side.[39] So, VW's unions and German government entities might justify their collaboration with unethical action at the company by referencing the positive effect of the Japanese government's corporate-friendly policies on Toyota. Similarly, fear of liberals, socialists, and communists prompted German conservative support of Hitler in 1932–33 and McConnell and Graham's 2020 support of Trump policies that they would have rejected based on their core principles. In all these cases, even if the aims of the collaborators weren't in line with the aims of the harm doers, the collaborators were responsible for enabling the harm doers to achieve their goals.

Ordinary Complicity

Benefiting from Privilege

In 2015, enrollment at the School for International Studies (SIS), a public middle and high school in Cobble Hill, Brooklyn, was dangerously low. There were just thirty students in the sixth grade, though the school could accommodate one hundred. The principal, Jillian Juman, was worried, she told reporter Chana Joffe-Walt, who traced the history of SIS for her podcast *Nice White Parents*.[1] With school funding based on enrollment, fewer students meant fewer resources. Juman was concerned that the New York City Department of Education might close SIS's middle school.

Cobble Hill had gentrified in recent years, but hardly any of the wealthy white families who lived near SIS sent their children there. Most SIS students were from working-class and poor families. Eighty-two percent were Black or Latino, and there was a sizable Middle Eastern population as well. Three-quarters of the students qualified for free lunches, and in 2014, fewer than 10 percent met grade-level standards for math and reading.[2] Parents could choose from a number of public middle schools for their kids, but most white parents in the

neighborhood focused on just three of them, all of which had relatively high test scores and significant white enrollment. But these three schools were overcrowded, with few openings, so parents needed to explore other options.

After Juman reached out to neighborhood families, white parents started touring SIS. Many expressed concern about the school's test scores and asked Juman, who is Black, if kids brought weapons to school. But they were impressed by its music program and enhanced academic curriculum, according to Joffe-Walt.

After touring SIS, a white Cobble Hill parent named Rob Hansen asked Juman if she'd consider starting a dual-language French program, similar to the one at his kids' elementary school. She told him she was open to the idea.

Hansen spread the news to friends in the neighborhood that SIS was starting a French program. He then sent some interested parents a survey to determine whether a significant number would commit to the school. Otherwise, he told Joffe-Walt, there would be the risk of what he called a "collective action problem": the possibility that only a very small number of kids from the neighborhood—white kids—would enroll. Hansen said he wanted to make sure the French program could run. Another white father, Stephen Leone, told New York–based news site DNAInfo that it was up to families like his to "create more good schools" because no one would do it for them. Seeing value in sending "an overflow of kids in bulk" to SIS, he joined Hansen in actively recruiting families to send their kids to SIS.[3]

Through their lobbying, parents like Hansen and Leone met their goal: a whopping 103 students enrolled in the sixth grade at SIS in 2015, up from 30. Almost all of the new kids were white.

Before the new white families arrived, the SIS PTA had focused primarily on community building: teacher appreciation activities, a spring carnival. By contrast, some of the new parents wanted to make fundraising a high priority, particularly to support the new French program. As it happened, Hansen was a professional fundraiser. He formed a parent fundraising committee independent of the PTA and set a short-term goal of raising $50,000.

At an October PTA meeting, Principal Juman announced that the new fundraising committee had already raised $18,000. Imee Hernandez, copresident of the SIS PTA, was confused. "So, can we use that money?" she asked. "Who's got it? And where's it going?" Rob Hansen wasn't a PTA officer, she noted. "Usually," she said, "money raised by parents goes through the PTA, so we can talk about where to spend it."[4] Hernandez's husband, Maurice, said that teachers had asked for new gym uniforms and microscopes. Could the new funds be used to meet these needs?

Hansen apologized for not communicating better with the PTA. He then shared that the French embassy in New York had offered about $10,000 to help pay for the French teachers and books. The embassy also wanted to throw a fundraiser for SIS.

"The fundraiser will be at the school, though, right?" asked Imee Hernandez. "And free, for everyone?" That was how SIS events had always been in the past, to accommodate low-income families and working parents' busy schedules: free, inclusive, convenient.

"Yes," said Hansen.

"Free? I just want to make sure everyone can go," Hernandez emphasized. Other parents nodded.

"Totally," said Hansen. "This is a community event, for our community."[5]

At the next PTA meeting, Hansen suggested keeping his new committee's fundraising efforts separate from the PTA, even as he insisted that the money he was raising would be for the school as a whole, not just the French program. Maurice Hernandez countered that it seemed "naive" to expect that the French embassy would agree to donate money for new chalkboards.

In a subsequent conversation with Joffe-Walt and Principal Juman, Rob Hansen said he wanted to establish a school-based foundation at SIS called the Brooklyn World Project. Private donors such as the French embassy, he said, wanted to have a say in how their money would be spent—just as Maurice Hernandez had anticipated. Funneling the money through the SIS PTA might thwart that goal by giving parents too much of a voice, Hansen explained.

At a PTA meeting, a parent named Deb who belonged to Hansen's fundraising committee gave an update on the French embassy's fundraiser for SIS. Her contact at the embassy said that the "gala," as it was now being called, had to be held in Manhattan rather than at SIS in Brooklyn or else donors wouldn't attend. "It's their event," Deb explained. "It's not really our event." The embassy was inviting 22,000 people. For security reasons, guests would have to be on a list and formally RSVP. While SIS parents could get in for free, the invitation would suggest a donation. After listing some of the donated items to be auctioned—including a stay at a four-bedroom home in Sonoma, California—Deb asked the parents at the PTA meeting to consider donating tickets to Broadway shows and New York Knicks games. Joffe-Walt described some of the parents looking at each other as if to say, "We're in the wrong room, right? How do we get out?" Imee Hernandez wasn't present, but Joffe-Walt recalled her trying to gently explain to a new

SIS parent why it might be hard for some families to pay $5 for classroom supplies.

In the view of PTA copresident Susan Moesker, who is white, some of the new white parents had a savior mentality toward SIS. "Here they come to save our poor struggling school that couldn't possibly make it on its own without their money and vision," she told Joffe-Walt, adding, "and we do not all feel that that is, necessarily, the case." The new parents' attitude may have rubbed off on some of their children. One sixth-grade boy told Joffe-Walt that SIS used to be a bad school where "the kids wouldn't pay attention" and likely "learned very little." Since he and his (white) friends arrived, he said, SIS had gone "really high up in the statuses."

The French embassy held its gala for SIS at its stately, ivy-covered Cultural Services Building in Manhattan, facing Central Park. Few SIS parents made the trek to the Upper East Side; most guests were well-heeled Francophiles with no connection to SIS. Fabrice Germain, the embassy representative, described its investment in SIS to Joffe-Walt as a form of "soft power." Looking "dumbstruck," PTA leader Moesker said it was "hard to explain how this is a public-school fundraiser."[6]

The gala raised money for the French program at SIS, but it left many parents deeply concerned about the direction the school was headed. SIS had adopted a French program simply because a white parent had proposed it and the principal had gone along. Many SIS families already spoke Spanish or Arabic, in addition to English. Why hadn't a dual-language Spanish or Arabic program that would empower minority students been considered? "There was money for a French program, which meant that at SIS, French had value," says Joffe-Walt. "Arabic didn't. Spanish didn't." Joffe-Walt concluded her podcast by noting that when integration occurs in the highly

segregated New York City school system, white parents will often "charge ahead, will sometimes be careless, secretive, or entitled," perhaps because they have little experience "sharing public schools." They may be so focused on what they believe will be best for their own children that they don't think about how others will be affected by the changes they bring about.

The ironic title of Joffe-Walt's podcast, *Nice White Parents*, refers to well-intentioned progressives—people who value diversity but may be unaware of the ways their power and bias make them complicit in harm inflicted on people of color. Throughout SIS's history—and indeed, the history of New York's public school system, Joffe-Walt argues—white parents have wielded their power to influence key decisions in favor of their interests, while the concerns of Black and brown parents have been systematically ignored and dismissed. "Just the very idea of us, the threat of our displeasure, warps the whole system," concludes Joffe-Walt (who is white).[7] It is easy to imagine that these "nice white parents" had good intentions for the school overall but that their privilege and bias toward their own children's interests prevented them from seeing the inequity in the changes and processes they put into motion.

Blind Spots That Affect the Rest of Us

Nearly all of us abhor racism and strive to treat others fairly and equally, regardless of their skin color. Today there are few overt racists. At the same time, all of us must function within systems that are inherently racist. Many of our educational, legal, and governmental systems, as well as corporations and nonprofits, were founded in times when little thought was given to treating people fairly across race and gender lines, and overt discrimination was common. And while many of those systems have taken

significant steps toward becoming less racist (in part because the law compels them to), they aren't close to the finish line. That's in part because our systems and organizations continue to privilege white people in subtle and not-so-subtle ways. And when we benefit from a racist system, we can become complicit in it and resist systemic change.

In this way, the New York City school system is a microcosm of the United States, which was set up, both implicitly and explicitly, to keep whites in power and other racial groups out of power. To begin with, most of us live on land taken from Native Americans. We think of slavery as a Southern institution, but the North was complicit in slavery. Over 40,000 Blacks were enslaved in the North in the mid-1700s, writes Anne Farrow in her book *Complicity: How the North Promoted, Prolonged, and Profited from Slavery*.[8] Northern Rhode Island was the center of the colonial slave trade, and the cotton produced in the South with slave labor was the "national currency, the product most responsible for America's explosive growth in the decades before the Civil War," according to Farrow.[9]

That might seem like ancient history, but many laws, government agencies, and private organizations continue to privilege whites, whether intentionally and overtly or not. Redlining, mortgage discrimination, and other racist housing practices kept Blacks from moving into prosperous neighborhoods—or actively pushed them out—where they might have accumulated family wealth through the appreciation of their homes. The GI Bill of 1944 funded college for hundreds of thousands of veterans, but because Black veterans were largely funneled into segregated vocational schools and blocked from four-year colleges, they were unable to reap the educational and career gains of white veterans.[10] Segregation has put white children in higher-quality schools, teeing them up for opportunities and

success, and Black children in underfunded and neglected schools in more dangerous neighborhoods, where chances for advancement are few.

Even the U.S. tax code, which we might assume to be color-blind, is indirectly racist. The code offers favorable tax treatment to those who sell their home at a profit, a structure that privileges whites, who are much more likely than Blacks to live in neighborhoods where homes appreciate significantly in value.[11] And the mortgage interest deduction, which allows Americans to deduct from their tax obligation interest paid to lenders on any properties they own, is a "massive subsidy" for wealthier Americans, who tend to be white, notes Heather McGhee in her book *The Sum of Us: What Racism Costs Everyone and How We Can Prosper Together.*[12] Bias and racism are also woven into the organizations we work for and the schools we attend. In a 2004 study, résumés with white-sounding names received 50 percent more callbacks than the same résumés with Black-sounding names.[13] And in a study of my industry, faculty members at top U.S. universities were significantly more open to meeting with white males who contacted them via email to talk about research opportunities than with women and people of color.[14]

That's a snapshot of just a few of the many advantages we white people receive—advantages that have snowballed over centuries into pernicious inequities. Yet we're often unaware of how we've benefited from racism and how our own behavior is complicit with racism. When we pass our wealth on through the generations, thanks in part to favorable tax treatment, the appreciation of our homes, and educational and career advantages, we unintentionally contribute to solidifying racial inequities. When we unintentionally give added advantage to the privileged by recommending our well-off white friends or their

children for jobs, we are failing to think about who doesn't have this kind of access and is being overlooked. And when we create and fund schools and school programs that primarily serve white kids, we are worsening racial disparities in the education system.

While action is needed by governments and corporations— from reforming the tax code to improving representation of Blacks in leadership roles—we can all work toward leveling the playing field. For white parents, this might mean bringing a new idea to the PTA for discussion rather than pushing it on the school administration in private. It might mean ensuring that members of other racial and ethnic groups are represented, and the impact on them considered carefully, whenever key decisions are made. It might mean noticing what's admirable about an unfamiliar culture and worth preserving. And it might mean approaching a new situation with humility and a willingness to learn rather than with certainty that you have the answers.

Our (My) Failure to Notice Privilege

In 1990, at the age of thirty-four, I was a visiting fellow at the Center for Advanced Study in the Behavioral Sciences in Stanford, California, on leave from my faculty position with Northwestern University's Kellogg Graduate School of Management. The center was loosely connected to Stanford University, and I spent part of my time during the fellowship around faculty in both the Stanford Center for Conflict Resolution and the Psychology Department. Stanford's Psychology Department was arguably the best in the world, and many of world's leading social psychologists, including Lee Ross, were on its faculty. I was invited to give a talk as part of the department's weekly seminar series. Lee was the host of my talk and would introduce me.

Before I explain what happened at the talk, a little background is needed. Lee had advised many doctoral students who went on to impressive academic careers. Not long before my talk, one of Lee's doctoral students had received and accepted an offer from a leading business school for a position as a first-year assistant professor. At that point in time, and to this day, business school professors were compensated far better than psychology professors, even within the same university. Business schools tend to be better funded than psychology departments. And as business schools experienced dramatic growth in the 1980s and 1990s, they lacked qualified applicants for faculty positions. In contrast, there was a backlog of highly qualified psychology PhDs looking for jobs in psychology departments. The jobs are similar, but not the same. Business school professors tend to teach more applied classes, for instance, including classes for MBA and executive students, which are lucrative to universities. Many graduating doctoral students in psychology programs consider the pay differential when deciding whether to apply for jobs in business schools. Meanwhile, psychology professors generally view offers from psychology departments as more prestigious than offers from business schools. Most psychology professors do not want to switch to business schools in order to obtain the higher pay. Still, back in 1990, the facts were clear: Lee was one of the most famous psychologists in the world, and he was twenty years into his career—yet his student's starting salary at a business school was higher than what Lee was earning.[15]

I was very excited, and a little nervous, to be giving a talk at Stanford's famous Psychology Department. I was speaking about inconsistencies in how people assess social comparisons when pay is unequal—how we tend to focus more on how our pay compares to that of others when we evaluate one job

opportunity at a time, and more on our own compensation when we compare two or more job opportunities.[16] As I recall, Lee's introduction was very gracious but ended with him expressing the hope that I would clarify why business school professors were paid so much more than psychology professors—a remark that certainly caught me off guard. In the middle of the seminar, Lee asked his question again. I passed up the opportunity to explain to this audience of psychologists, with a few business school professors sprinkled in, how the heightened demand from business schools dictated that B-school professors ended up earning far more than others doing similar work. When the seminar was over, Lee publicly thanked me for a very nice talk but noted that I never really provided useful insight into the pay differential that was on his mind.

That evening, I went out to dinner with the Stanford social psychology faculty, including Lee, and the department's doctoral students. After enjoying Indian food in Mountain View, a small quiet town near Stanford at the time, which looked nothing like the Mountain View that is now the center of Silicon Valley, we returned to the Psychology Department for a smaller group discussion of the work I'd presented that day. Along with being brilliant, Lee was often animated and talkative. Once the discussion was underway, Lee returned to his theme of the day, this time focused on what annoyed him about me: he believed that the pay differential he'd highlighted was a grave injustice, but as far as he could tell, I had never even thought about it. Why was I so negligent in caring about this issue?

Like most business school professors, I simply accepted that our job market was stronger than that of psychology professors for the reasons described above. And I knew that high-quality research psychologists like Lee could easily obtain very well-paid positions if they were willing to teach in business schools.

From Lee's perspective, the differential was unfair, given that the jobs were so similar and we worked for the same universities. And in many countries, all professors at the same level earn the same pay, regardless of their area of expertise. But Lee was correct: I had never viewed the differential as an injustice. He had.

We spent the rest of the evening discussing this topic. We talked about the underlying psychological factors that would explain why B-school and psychology professors seemed to have different perspectives on the pay differential. And we thought about how to study the issue—particularly, the fact that while Lee and I both studied social comparisons, he was obsessed with the injustice of the pay differential, and I had given it little thought. The discussion led Lee and me to conduct multiple experiments, along with Kristina Diekmann and Steve Samuels (advisees of ours at the time),[17] which showed that people focus more on inequality when they are disadvantaged than when they are advantaged (or privileged). We also found that people are psychologically willing to accept advantage that others provide them at levels they would never claim for ourselves. Thus, I accepted my higher pay as a business school faculty member without thinking about the inequality. This was true despite the fact that if I had been asked at the time what the appropriate pay differential should be between psychology and business school professors, I probably would have said that it should be lower than it was. Clearly, I had a motivation not to look at the pay discrepancy too closely, as doing so might have required me to accept that I was the beneficiary of privilege. In other words, I was complicit in the inequality. If I hadn't been prompted by Lee's questions, I likely wouldn't have thought deeply about the discrepancy to this day.

Admittedly, the question of whether well-paid psychology professors are disadvantaged relative to better-paid business

school professors is rooted in privilege. Like most of our colleagues at the time, and many of them to this day, Lee and I were both white males who did not face career roadblocks as a result of our race or gender. But the psychology that we uncovered behind our different perceptions of the pay discrepancy has broader implications for more significant societal issues related to injustice.

If you had asked me just a few years ago whether I was privileged, I would have bristled at the term. I've maintained a self-image as a gritty city kid from Pittsburgh. I take pride in having earned all of my own spending money in my teen years as a ballpark vendor (Pirates, Steelers, Pitt Panthers). I also paid for most of college with many part-time jobs, and to save a year of tuition, I overloaded on courses each term and graduated from the University of Pennsylvania in three years. To me, it was my contemporaries from wealthy families, the ones who didn't have to work or rush through school, who were privileged.

My views on privilege changed in 2018 when I read the book *The Person You Mean to Be: How Good People Fight Bias* by my friend and coauthor Dolly Chugh.[18] Building on the ideas of antiracist educator and author Debby Irving, Dolly uses the metaphor of tailwinds and headwinds to explain the invisible advantages that many of us enjoy while others have invisible forces pushing against them. The notion that I have benefited from many tailwinds in my life, while others were held back by headwinds, is both obviously true and easy to accept. That is, I have been privileged relative to others, particularly women and people of color. Even those of us who believe that we have earned our role and status should be aware that there are many factors outside of our control that enabled our success. When we fail to see our privilege, we risk becoming complicit with existing structures that breed inequality.

The Privilege of Recognizing Others

In my industry, academia, professors receive credit and prestige for our publications, teaching, and service. Academia is enthusiastic about honoring people with awards, far more than in most industries. When I receive an award, I appreciate the recognition of my past work and feel proud. However, until I was well into the writing of this book, I had never stopped to question whether I was the most appropriate person to receive the award or to question the processes that academics have created to choose award recipients. I never stopped to ask whether my privilege gave me an unfair advantage in the award decision process.

This began to change in the fall of 2020, when I got an email from Dolly Chugh. Dolly had recently received an email from the American Psychological Society (APS) announcing that the nomination period had opened for the APS Rising Star award. The award is presented to outstanding psychological scientists in the earliest stages of their post-PhD research careers. "I'm catching up on emails," Dolly wrote to me regarding the APS nomination announcement, "and realizing this is an opportunity to support an underrepresented scholar who might not typically be recognized for her significant contributions to the field." She encouraged me to help her come up with possible nominees. I was happy to join Dolly's thoughtful effort.

Together, Dolly and I sent in nominations for a specific underrepresented scholar. That person did not receive the award. I was mildly disappointed, but I didn't have a clear assessment of how our nominee compared to the other scholars who had been nominated, and I didn't know much about the APS nomination process. I still felt a small amount of satisfaction for having been involved in the search, in large part due to Dolly's nudge.

A half year later, on February 20, 2021, I received an annual request for nominations for the Fellows Group of the Academy of Management, the leading association for management and organization scholars. The Fellows Group, an honorific society I belong to, is made up of about 1 percent of the 20,000 members of the academy, most of whom are professors in business schools throughout the world. According to the academy, the purpose of the Fellows Group is "to recognize and honor members of the Academy of Management who have made significant contributions to the science and practice of management, and to provide opportunities for fellowship and a forum for discussion among persons so recognized and honored." In response to prior annual requests from the Fellows Group, I had occasionally nominated people, usually former doctoral advisees of mine. Each existing member could nominate one new member a year or simply ignore the announcement.

The Fellows Group holds an annual meeting, which, pre-COVID, was a dinner held each summer during the Academy of Management's annual conference. I attended the dinners irregularly; when I did, it was nice to see many old friends. The dinner was typically sponsored at a nice location, and it included tributes to the members who had passed away (an indication of the membership's demographics), the induction of newly elected members, and the chance to network and see friends. As far as the Fellows Group's activities go, that's about it. I didn't notice that most of the attendees at these dinners were white, though that was undoubtedly the case. (One of my Black colleagues has pointed out that she never fails to notice race when she is the only Black person at an academic gathering.) I also don't ever recall a discussion about improving the racial diversity of the Fellows Group, and I never initiated such a conversation myself.

Dolly's email from six months before prompted me to consider the race and gender of my doctoral students. All of the students for whom I served as the dissertation chair at the Kellogg School of Management from 1985 to 2000 were white (most were female). This hasn't been true in the new millennium while I've been at Harvard, but many of my nominees were from my time at Kellogg. I think that all of my former nominees for the Fellows Group were also white. So, with Dolly's email in mind, I decided to search for scholars from underrepresented communities. I nominated an excellent scholar and leader whose profile was not typical of Fellows Group nominees. Like Fellows whom I nominated in the past, her research is top quality. But unlike others, she had taken on senior administrative assignments at her universities rather than just focusing on academic publications.

The screening committee of the Fellows Group assessed the twenty nominations it received in 2021 and forwarded fifteen on for formal voting by the membership. My nominee didn't make it past the initial screen. I was disappointed, as I was convinced that the nominee's overall credentials far exceeded the bar. At the same time, I recognized that I had failed to consider the homogeneity of my previous nominations until my most recent nominee had been passed over. For years, my complicity contributed to the homogeneous set of Fellows.

It was time for me to learn more about the process and think about my complicity. For the first time, I went back and carefully read the nomination process. I learned that as of April 2021, there was only one Black Fellow in the group, representing .005 percent of the Academy of Management's membership. I could easily come up with many Black scholars with research records that were on a par with, or exceeded, those of current Fellows.

I now recognized that the selection process was one that I would not recommend to any organization that valued diversity. Under the existing process, the almost entirely white and, until fairly recently, primarily male membership required a nomination from an existing member. Nominees were frequently good friends or close colleagues of existing members. Social science research highlights that this is a formula for perpetuating the existing demographics—people tend to socialize and recommend people who are like themselves. In addition, asking for one name, as the Academy of Management had done—particularly from a white male membership—would further restrict diversity. Organizations are more likely to achieve diversity when they ask people to nominate many candidates rather than fewer, research shows.[19]

Had it not been for Dolly's email about a different award, I could have easily continued to fail to notice the homogeneity of the Fellows Group. I believe many other current Fellows would say the same, including those who have published, taught, and consulted on the topic of inclusion and diversity. Our failure can be partly explained by the widespread human tendency to accept systems as they currently exist, particularly when our group is favored by those systems. When we fail to think about, notice, and act on how these legacy systems create bias, we are complicit.

One of the most common ways in which we fail to notice our complicity is when we accept unequal, privileged, and unethical behaviors that are built into existing systems. When we accept restrictions on mail-in voting, try to justify immoral preferences for well-connected candidates at elite universities, or discuss how a recruit will "fit" into our majority-white organization, we are preventing the injustice of such practices from being discussed in our organizations. Too many actors create

and foster environments that can be predicted to lead others to engage in destructive behaviors. And far too many of us accept the existing system as the way the world works rather than asking how we can change the structures that lead to unethical action.

Because silence and ignorance in the face of racism are just another form of complicity, those of us with privilege need to educate ourselves on the history of racism in our country and communities, learn about implicit bias, and find out more about how whites have benefited from racism. Without that knowledge, our privilege may not be apparent to us. We also need to embark on the challenging work of making less biased decisions, supporting more equitable policies, and speaking up against racist behaviors and practices. This might at times appear to require sacrifices, but those "sacrifices" will often have great long-term payoffs for all. In her book *The Sum of Us: What Racism Costs Everyone and How We Can Prosper Together*, economic and social policy expert Heather McGhee argues that in every significant realm of life, from housing to education to employment to climate change, white people would often benefit from reductions in systemic racism.[20] That is, she convincingly refutes the widespread belief that progress for Blacks must come at the expense of whites. As a metaphor, McGhee describes how, in response to desegregation during the 1950s, many predominantly white U.S. towns closed their community swimming pools. In place of this mutually harmful zero-sum mindset, she argues, we can achieve "solidarity dividends" by implementing policy interventions aimed at reducing racial disparities in health, education, incarceration, and jobs. According to a 2020 report by Citigroup, if gaps between Black and white Americans in wages, housing, education, and investment had closed in the year 2000, $16 trillion could have been added

to the U.S. economy—dividends that could still be achieved in the years ahead.[21]

Failing to think about our privilege often leads us to be complicit when bad things happen—even with events that feel distant from our own actions. Privilege should make it easier for us to speak up for justice. After all, those of us with privilege typically risk very little when we do so—not our jobs, our homes, or our freedom. Through greater reflection and a willingness to change, we can better align our behavior with our higher ethical standards.

5

Believing in a False Prophet

Larry Layton grew up as a Quaker and pacifist, attended Berkeley High School in Northern California, and was the editor of a campus newspaper called *The Liberal*. After graduating from the University of California, Davis, in 1968, Layton and his wife, Carolyn, moved farther north to the Ukiah area and, eager to work for social justice, joined the Peoples Temple, a church that combined elements of Christianity and socialism with communal living. Layton was attracted to the Temple's utopian principles and multiracial community.[1] The Temple was led by the charismatic Reverend Jim Jones, who presented himself as a faith healer and leftist political prophet. Layton viewed the Temple as a civil rights movement and compared Jones to Martin Luther King Jr.[2]

In the mid-1970s, facing media investigations, Jim Jones fled to Guyana along with hundreds of his followers, including the Laytons, and established a settlement known as Jonestown. There, Jones set his sights on Carolyn Layton. Jones told Larry that he wanted Carolyn to be one of his romantic partners. Both Larry and Carolyn Layton complied, and she left Larry for

Jones's harem. Layton remarried, but Jones became attracted to his new wife as well, and she too left Layton for Jones's harem. Larry Layton nonetheless remained a loyal follower of Jones.

The Peoples Temple grew to become perhaps the most dangerous cult in history, with members accused of committing numerous crimes, including kidnapping and rape. The approximately 900 members of the cult were not free to leave the Guyana campsite. Concerns over what was happening to American citizens in Guyana led U.S. congressman Leo Ryan to visit Jonestown in November 1978. Some members of the community told Ryan that they wanted to return to the States and were not being allowed to do so. Jones viewed these reports as acts of betrayal. As Ryan prepared to leave the country with some of the cult members, he, one of the defectors, and three journalists were shot to death by Temple gunmen on the airstrip. Layton, who had been posing as a defector, wounded two people at the airstrip and was arrested.

Jones recognized that the cold-blooded murders would guarantee the demise of the church. That evening, insisting that they were at risk of imminent attack, he instructed his followers to commit "revolutionary suicide" by drinking cyanide-laced punch (which led to the well-known saying "drinking the Kool-Aid," though Flavor Aid was the brand used).[3] Jones's most militaristic members acted as armed guards to ensure that no one fled. Parents gave the poison to their children to drink and lay down beside them before killing themselves. The bodies of Jones and 912 cult members, 304 of them children, were soon discovered. Only 80 members of the cult in Jonestown survived the massacre.

After the Jonestown massacre, Temple survivors, some continuing to believe in the prophecy of Jim Jones, struggled to return to anything resembling normal life. A string of

violent incidents followed. In 1979, Jonestown survivor Mike Prokes, who had managed media relations for the cult, held a press conference in a Modesto, California, hotel room, where he complained of federal harassment in connection with the Jonestown massacre, arguing, "These people did not die in vain."[4] Prokes then went into the bathroom and shot himself, dying soon after. Al and Jeannie Mills, who defected from the church and were openly critical of it, were murdered in their Berkeley, California, home in 1980. Laurence Mann, a former Guyanese ambassador to the United States, murdered his long-time companion, former Temple staff member Paula Adams, and their child and then killed himself. In 1984, Tyrone Mitchell, who lost parents and siblings in Jonestown, opened fire on a Los Angeles schoolyard from his house across the street, killing two people and injuring twelve others, and then killed himself.

As for Layton, he was convicted of conspiracy in the murder of Ryan and his party. He and hundreds of others clearly suffered from their decision to follow Jones, yet they were also complicit in the horror he created. Most entered the church with good motives, believed in civil rights, and were idealistic, well-intentioned people. Many also moved their families to Guyana, where they engaged in and enforced authoritarian, sexist, and barbaric practices.

The Pull of Charismatic Leaders

Most people who develop a faith in a false prophet do not go on to participate in a tragedy like Jonestown, yet many false prophets lead their followers to commit harm. How do we explain this behavior?

Obviously, members of the Peoples Temple had faith, which can be defined as a strong or unshakable belief that exists

without proof or evidence. While some may disagree with this particular definition of faith, it is broadly consistent with the writings of those who see a distinction between action based on faith versus action based on reason.[5] Reason implies a deliberative cognitive process; faith sometimes requires the suppression of such deliberation. Some view the need to deliberate as evidence of a lack of faith.

I want to emphasize that I am not opposed to faith. I have faith in lots of people. I have learned to trust many people who know more than I do about a lot of things. When they tell me something is a fact or a scientifically proven result, I move forward with faith in their judgment, as I often lack the time or expertise to fully deliberate about their claim. Notably, my faith in their expertise and integrity is something that I have developed over time, and the vast majority of these individuals would have no interest in suppressing my own deliberation. But relying on faith comes with risks.

When people try to keep us from deliberating, we should be concerned. When business consultants urge us to implement their advice based on our faith in their expertise but don't share information that would allow us to deliberate along with them, we should be suspicious. Similarly, while I honestly have no interest in getting you to question your faith in the existence of God or the worthiness of any particular religious figures, I do become suspicious when religions or religious figures command devotion at the expense of deliberation. I don't know why any source of inspiration that values integrity would want us to think less rather than more.

People are often inspired and affected by leaders with charisma, defined as the ability to influence others and attract their attention and admiration. Leaders with charisma often have a remarkable ability to influence the belief systems of individuals,

communities, companies, and nations. Some charismatic leaders, including Abraham Lincoln, Gandhi, and Martin Luther
King Jr., are admired for doing good. But there can be a distinct
dark side to charismatic leadership. Jim Jones had much in
common with David Koresh, leader of the Branch Davidian
cult, which came to an end during a bloody standoff in Waco,
Texas, in 1993. Donald Trump, Adam Neumann, and Elizabeth
Holmes are other charismatic leaders who attracted a cult or
cult-like following. When such leaders commit evil or otherwise act against the interests of society, the suppression of
deliberation by their adherents can cause massive damage.

People under the sway of a charismatic leader often accept
their views unquestioningly, losing their grip on reality in the
process. This blind adherence can have tragic outcomes, as
was the case in Jonestown. In political contexts, deference to
charismatic leaders can threaten democracy and bring about
totalitarianism. The state-controlled Soviet press churned out
loving characterizations of Stalin, describing him as "great,"
"beloved," "bold," "wise," and "genius."[6] The Communist Party
portrayed Stalin, whose collectivization policies and repression
led to the deaths of millions of Russians and others, as a caring
and strong father to the Soviet people. In the United States,
Trump's attempt to discredit the results of the 2020 election,
which he lost, culminated tragically in his followers' attempts to
overthrow the government on January 6, 2021. In the corporate
world, as we'll see, deference to a charismatic leader may enable
incompetence, abuse, and unethical and illegal behaviors.

When Walgreens Executives Fell for a False Prophet

In 2004, after dropping out of Stanford at age nineteen, Elizabeth Holmes founded Theranos, a company she claimed would

revolutionize the blood-testing process. According to Holmes, she'd developed a breakthrough technology that was faster, more accurate, less invasive, and cheaper than the traditional strategy of using a syringe to draw blood. The technology—a small, portable machine—could conduct up to two hundred different blood tests with less than one one-hundredth of the amount of blood taken using traditional blood samples, she claimed. Theranos raised over $700 million from early-stage investors. By 2014, the company had peaked at a market value of over $9 billion; Holmes owned more than half of that amount.

In October 2015, the *Wall Street Journal* published an article by reporter John Carreyrou that raised doubts about the effectiveness of Theranos's technology and revealed that the company used traditional machines produced by competitors to conduct the vast majority of the blood tests it handled.[7] Eventually, Carreyrou reported that Holmes had misled Theranos's investors and board members with numerous fraudulent claims. The most significant fabrication was that the Theranos technology actually worked. A variety of legal and commercial challenges followed, which are documented in Carreyrou's book *Bad Blood*.[8] By 2016, Holmes's personal net worth had dropped from over $4.5 billion to virtually nothing. In March 2018, federal prosecutors brought charges of fraud against her, Theranos, and Ramesh "Sunny" Balwani (the company's former president and Holmes's romantic partner at the time). Holmes stood accused of falsely stating that the company had $100 million in annual revenue, when in fact annual revenues were under $100,000. This was just one of the hundreds of lies that Holmes and Balwani had told investors, the board, and commercial partners. Holmes resolved civil charges by paying a fine of $500,000, returning her 18.9 million shares of Theranos, and giving up control of the company. She was

barred from serving as a director or officer of any public company for the next decade. In 2018, the U.S. attorney for Northern California indicted Holmes and Balwani on wire fraud and conspiracy charges.[9] The company dissolved on September 4, 2018. On January 3, 2022, a federal jury found Holmes guilty of four of eleven fraud charges, including wire fraud and conspiracy to commit wire fraud. The verdict suggested jurors believed Holmes lied about Theranos's technology, though they were deadlocked on charges related to defrauding investors and did not convict her for defrauding patients. "The verdict stands out for its rarity," the *New York Times* reports. "Few technology executives are charged with fraud and even fewer are convicted."[10]

Standing out from the sea of men in Silicon Valley, Holmes created a facade that allowed her to fool employees, investors, and board members for years. When people in her entourage started comparing her to Apple founder Steve Jobs, she started dressing like him, in black turtlenecks and slacks. Theranos CFO Henry Mosley, whom Holmes fired for bringing up the fact that Theranos had been conning investors, described the twenty-two-year-old Theranos founder like this:

> She had the presence of someone much older than she was. The way she trained her big blue eyes on you without blinking made you feel like the center of the world. It was almost hypnotic. Her voice added to the mesmerizing effect: she spoke in an unusually deep baritone.[11]

Holmes was one of *Time* magazine's 100 most influential people and *Glamour* magazine's "Woman of the Year" in 2015. Many viewed her as brilliant, visionary, charming, and a prophet of the future of medicine. Venture capital firms, Theranos employees and board members, and business partners all flocked to

Holmes and followed her prophecies of financial success and medical breakthroughs.

One of those mindless complicitors was the drugstore giant Walgreens. On August 24, 2010, a Walgreens team descended on Theranos's Palo Alto headquarters for a two-day discussion of a pilot project in which Walgreens would use Theranos's technology in its pharmacies. The head of the Walgreens team, Dr. Jay Rosan—known as "Dr. J"—had been charged with finding new technologies that could reboot the aging pharmacy chain. Theranos's technology appeared to offer a true competitive advantage for Walgreens in its fierce competition with CVS. Under the deal, Walgreens would pay up to $50 million for cartridges to be used in Theranos blood-testing equipment at a small number of the chain's pharmacies and loan the start-up another $25 million. Holmes promised Walgreens that customers would be able to have their fingers pricked at the stores and get results for up to two hundred different blood tests within an hour. If the pilot program went well, the companies hoped to expand their partnership nationwide.

One member of the Walgreens negotiating team was Kevin Hunter, the owner of Collaborate, a small lab consulting firm that Walgreens had hired to evaluate Theranos's technology and the partnership. Hunter repeatedly asked to see Theranos's laboratory facilities, one level down; Holmes said that wouldn't be possible. Holmes and Balwani also refused to conduct a blood test on Hunter and Dr. J, which Hunter had arranged to compare to a test taken using a conventional blood draw at nearby Stanford Medical Center.

By the end of the first day of meetings, Hunter was highly suspicious of Holmes's claims. Dr. J, by contrast, seemed dazzled by both her and the Silicon Valley milieu. The next day, Walgreens CFO Wade Miquelton arrived, presold on the wisdom

of sealing an agreement he'd negotiated directly with Holmes. Hunter didn't understand why Walgreens was paying him for a scientific assessment its executives didn't seem to want. When he got home, he wrote up a report warning the Walgreens leaders that Theranos might be "overselling or overstating . . . where they are at scientifically with cartridges/devices."[12]

A month later, Holmes and Balwani visited Walgreens's headquarters in Deerfield, Illinois, to kick off Project Beta, the pilot program. After one of the Walgreens executives sang the Beatles song "Imagine" with new lyrics immortalizing the venture, Holmes and Balwani encouraged the executives, including Walgreens president Kermit Crawford, to have their fingers pricked, ostensibly so their blood could be tested with Theranos's technology. Hunter, who had begun working for Walgreens as a full-time on-site consultant, was hopeful that he would finally have a chance to see how the technology measured up to traditional blood tests. He requested the test results on a video call a few days later, but they never arrived. Hunter next proposed a systematic test of the Theranos technology. Holmes demurred.

Hunter presented these and other red flags surrounding Walgreens's $100-million-plus investment to Renaat Van den Hooff, the Walgreens executive overseeing the pilot project. Van den Hooff seemed shaken but said that if Theranos was legit, Walgreens couldn't risk the start-up choosing to partner instead with the pharmacy's chief rival, CVS. Notably, if Theranos's technology had been valid, Holmes would have wanted to provide clear evidence of that to Walgreens in hopes of negotiating an even more attractive deal. But Walgreens executives seemed to have put so much faith in Holmes that they had stopped thinking rationally about their negotiating counterpart's perspective.

Hunter continued to ask Holmes and Balwani probing questions on weekly video calls, to the point that they asked him to be shut out of meetings in early 2011. Walgreens complied, still fearful that Theranos would break off the deal and ally with CVS.

Walgreens eventually opened forty Theranos "wellness centers" at stores in Arizona and California that offered inexpensive finger-prick blood-test services for up to two hundred diagnoses. During his investigation, Carreyrou spoke to numerous doctors who believed Theranos provided inaccurate blood-test results to some of their patients who were tested at the wellness centers. In fact, Theranos provided invalid and sometimes alarming results to *thousands* of Walgreens customers—some of whom had grave illnesses, including cancer. Walgreens pressed Theranos for answers. But when Carreyrou reported in the *Wall Street Journal* in May 2016 that Theranos had voided tens of thousands of blood-test results, essentially admitting they could not be relied upon, Walgreens executives were somehow "astonished," despite the many signs of trouble.[13]

The pharmacy chain terminated its contract with Theranos on June 12, 2016, and closed all of the Theranos wellness centers in its stores. The following year, Theranos agreed to pay the state of Arizona $4.65 million to refund to anyone who had bought one of its Walgreens blood tests. Walgreens also sued Theranos for its $140 million investment; the companies reached a confidential settlement. "The partnership had a problem," Walgreens concluded in its lawsuit. "Theranos's revolutionary system was a blatant fraud."[14]

Walgreens's due-diligence failures and complete faith in Holmes's claims were striking. But Walgreens was just one of many complicitors who maintained faith in this false prophet even after glaring evidence of fraud emerged. The venture

capital funds that invested in Theranos failed to notice that Theranos avoided putting medical or biological experts on its board, people who would have known that Holmes's claims were physically impossible. Instead, Holmes packed the board with famous former U.S. government leaders who lacked medical expertise, including George Shultz, Henry Kissinger, General James Mattis, William Perry, and Sam Nunn. These illustrious men were somehow easily hoodwinked by Holmes and unconcerned about their own lack of relevant expertise. And they were complicit in Holmes's deception when they failed to take note of the many warning signs.

Leaders have an explicit obligation to provide the oversight needed to detect and act on potential problems facing their organizations. When they put faith in a charismatic personality, they may be deterred from meeting this responsibility.

Back to WeWork

WeWork CEO and founder Adam Neumann was another corporate prophet in the vein of Elizabeth Holmes. In chapter 3, we examined the role of some of WeWork's collaborators, the venture capital community, in Neumann's fraud. But his wrongdoing was also enabled by those who believed wholeheartedly in his false prophecies, including his employees.

A self-styled millennial prophet, Neumann presented WeWork as a social movement that could "elevate the world's consciousness" and solve our most difficult problems. Many people have described Neumann as the most convincing salesperson they'd ever met. "People were skeptical . . . but once you get in a room with him [and] listen to his vision, you get attracted," Noah Wintroub, vice chairman of investment banking at JPMorgan, told the *Financial Times*. "He's about as

magnetic in terms of charisma as anybody I've seen."[15] Neumann himself had delusions of grandeur, saying he wanted to be "president of the world," live forever, and become the first trillionaire.[16]

At the WeWork "summer camp" (company retreat) in 2013, Neumann told his employees that success would come from building "something that has intention." "Every one of us is here because it has meaning," he continued, "because we want to do something that actually makes the world a better place. And we want to make money doing it!"[17] Back at the office, Neumann encouraged a cult-like atmosphere, a corporate culture of mandatory admiration. "So many of the people were young and had never worked in a real company," one former WeWork senior executive told *Vanity Fair*. "They bought all of it. I realized after I got there it was a cult."[18]

Oddly enough for a real estate business, ego and mysticism were central to WeWork. Valuing faith over reason, Neumann squelched the use of analysis and logic. Standard economic principles wouldn't apply in the future "WeWorld," he believed. Neumann's spirituality and guru-like self-presentation were connected to his and his wife Rebekah's identification as followers of Kabbalah, a Jewish mystical faith. Kabbalah became part of the WeWork's office culture. Key meetings were often scheduled on the eighteenth of the month because eighteen is a sacred number in Kabbalah's thirty-two paths to wisdom. Neumann encouraged senior WeWork executives to attend study meetings with his spiritual adviser, Rabbi Eitan Yardeni, the company's "spiritual counselor."[19]

Neumann pitched WeWork as offering not just office space but a new way of working, living, and interacting with others. He encouraged his employees to "make a life and not just a living."[20] Employees put their faith in Neumann, working long

hours for low pay. Coworkers became friends, and work did indeed become life. "They pushed the narrative that this is your family, and you're supposed to spend a lot of time with them," one employee told *Vanity Fair*. "It was somewhat incestuous. It was like we were at war together."[21]

SoftBank's $4.4 billion investment enhanced Neumann's messianic stature. "Adam's fantasy land became a reality," one WeWork executive told *Vanity Fair*.[22] Neumann met with world leaders like Canadian prime minister Justin Trudeau and offered his views on the Syrian refugee crisis and other weighty topics. "When Adam got in front of world leaders, it was like he started thinking he was one," reported one WeWork executive.[23] Neumann rambled about WeWork solving the world's thorniest problems: "We could wake up one day" and "within two years" ensure that the world's 150 million orphans have families, he suggested.[24] "Then we can go to any minority, and anyone who is weaker, who is getting taken advantage of by someone who is more powerful," the next-generation messiah continued. "And from that we can go to world hunger."

Neumann didn't seem to be interested in fixing problems closer to home, such as how to ensure that WeWork's cleaners earned a living wage and had access to health-care benefits. Instead, he hired union-busting contractors. Although Neumann preached a gospel of aiding the less powerful, his actions suggested that his real god was money, which he sought by instilling blind faith in his employees. Thousands of them worked at below-market pay, believing they were helping to change the world and that their small equity stakes in the company would be their path to riches. Neumann dangled the promise of an IPO that would allow them to cash in, but his house of cards collapsed before that could happen. Instead, workers lost their jobs, their equity, their dream. "This company was designed

and managed to make a handful of people ungodly wealthy at the expense of everyone," one employee concluded.[25]

Those who blindly accepted Neumann's preaching were complicit in allowing the fraud to continue. The company's top leaders, investors, and board members were more complicit than lower-level employees. When the company collapsed, the employees were left without jobs and with worthless stock options. The Neumanns fled the United States as billionaires.

Why We Accept False Prophets

Cults are often defined as social groups with unconventional spiritual or philosophical beliefs, united by a particular personality, object, or goal.[26] Faith, meanwhile, tends to be defined by beliefs based on inspiration, revelation, or deference to authority. In religious contexts, faith often depends on acceptance of a miracle or the views of a specific person or deity. Clearly, faith is a core component of both formal religions and those deemed cults. While members of traditional religions are quick to separate themselves from cults, cult members often correctly note that both types of groups tend to believe in miracles that defy scientific reasoning to bolster their faith—it's just that the cults' miracles are more recent. Meanwhile, when people put their faith in new business propositions or a charismatic "prophet," they tend to assert that old business models no longer apply, or in the current jargon, they present themselves as "disrupters." Yet, too often, such enterprises lack evidence to support their claims and encourage the suppression of deliberation.

Religions, old and new, hold various views on the relationship between faith and reason. In the fourteenth century, the Jewish philosopher Levi ben Gerson tried to reconcile faith and reason by arguing that "the Torah cannot prevent us

from considering to be true that which our reason urges us to believe."[27] In contrast, his contemporary, Hasdai ben Abraham Crescas, countered that reason is weak and faith strong, and that faith alone will allow Jews to endure the suffering that is the common lot of God's chosen people.[28] The Quran repeatedly emphasizes the importance of thinking, rationality, and contemplation, exhorting Muslims to learn about the natural world.[29] The Christian Science movement, founded in nineteenth-century New England, holds that illness can only be cured through prayer and discourages members from receiving medical treatment. However, many Christian faiths embrace science and its beneficial applications. In a 1998 encyclical, Pope John Paul II wrote that faith and reason are not only compatible but also essential in the quest for truth.[30]

The distinction between faith and reason parallels the distinction made in the behavioral economics literature between two main types of thought, System 1 and System 2.[31] Nobel laureate Daniel Kahneman argues, based on earlier research by Keith Stanovich and Richard West,[32] that humans make decisions in two different modes. System 1 thinking is the system we use most of the time. System 1 is fast, automatic, and efficient. Decision researchers note that when we are using this intuitive system, we rely on a number of simplifying strategies, or rules of thumb, known as heuristics, to make decisions.[33] Because heuristics help us cope with the complex environment surrounding our decisions, they can be very helpful when we are making relatively trivial decisions, such as whether to put our left or right shoe on first, as well as split-second decisions, such as braking when a deer leaps in front of your car. By comparison, when we stop and deliberate—that is, when we reason—we engage in System 2 thinking, which is slower, more deliberate, more cognitive, and less reliant on general

rules of thumb. We benefit from using our System 2 thinking when making important decisions, such as whether to accept a job and whether to trust someone.

Putting faith in someone can be a heuristic, particularly if they haven't earned your faith. When we put our faith in leaders—whether religious, corporate, governmental, or otherwise—we have little need to deliberate. We do what they say not necessarily because it makes logical sense but because we have faith that they will provide us with wise direction. Charismatic leaders who encourage their followers to abandon reason—including Jim Jones, Elizabeth Holmes, and Adam Neumann—are particularly dangerous because they are so skilled at persuading people to accept their lies and look past their wrongdoing.

I continue to have faith in many people's judgment. Many of my doctoral advisees have known how to do part of a research project better than I could; rather than rechecking every piece of their work, I put my faith in their skills, integrity, and thoroughness. But this faith should be based on my reasoning from the evidence I gather about them, and none of these scholars have expected me to suppress my own reasoning to accept their views. In fact, they want me to engage my deliberation to understand their arguments. When people ask us to suppress our deliberation, we should be suspect. And when we defer to others based on faith without reasoning, we become complicit in their harmful acts. This temptation can be especially strong when those with power and authority expect our complicity.

6

Authority and Loyalty

In the entertainment world, it was an open secret for decades that film producer Harvey Weinstein was a serial predator, someone who habitually harassed and sexually assaulted women. "I know that everybody—I mean everybody—in Hollywood knows that it's happening," the French actor Emma de Caunes, who accused Weinstein of sexually harassing her in the Paris Ritz hotel in 2010, told reporter Ronan Farrow for an October 2017 *New Yorker* article. "He's not even really hiding."[1] Only after both the *New York Times* and the *New Yorker* published numerous firsthand accounts of Weinstein's behavior was he finally held accountable.[2] Eventually, more than ninety women came forward to accuse Weinstein of sexual harassment or assault. While serving twenty-three years in a New York State prison for sex crimes, in April 2021, Weinstein was indicted on eleven more counts of sexual assault in Los Angeles.

How was a serial rapist and harasser able to run loose in Hollywood, New York, Italy, France, and beyond for over twenty-five years? Weinstein created a "culture of complicity" within Miramax and The Weinstein Company (TWC), the

entertainment firms he cofounded and ran with his brother, Bob. "Almost everyone had incentives to look the other way or reasons to stay silent," journalists Megan Twohey and Jodi Kantor concluded in their 2017 *New York Times* article "Weinstein's Complicity Machine," for which they interviewed nearly two hundred people.[3] Those who knew about Weinstein's crimes stayed silent for various reasons. The producer was known for threatening, punishing, and firing employees who stood up to him, so fear was a key motivator for complicity. And some who worked for Weinstein kept quiet about the abuse or even aided him, simply because they deferred to his authority: Weinstein was the boss, and the boss gets to make the rules.

After speaking with dozens of Weinstein's accusers, Farrow concluded that the producer's crimes tended to follow a similar script and were enabled by a vast network of his employee-complicitors. Current and former assistants described how their boss enlisted them to lure aspiring female actors and models to business meetings or parties, often late at night at hotel bars or hotel rooms. After getting his prey alone, Weinstein might discuss business at first but eventually would try to coerce the woman to be intimate with him. If she refused, he would often sexually assault her. Afterward, assistants were often expected to lead these women away from the scene of the crime.

In 2004, one of Weinstein's assistants ushered dancer Ashley Matthau into a hotel room for what she'd been told was a business meeting with the producer. The assistant waited outside the door while Weinstein sexually assaulted Matthau. When Matthau emerged from the room, crying, the assistant didn't acknowledge her as they walked backed to hotel lobby. "It just seemed like a well-oiled machine," Matthau told the *Times*.[4] Also in 2004, aspiring actor Lucia Evans, expecting to read

for Weinstein and a Miramax casting executive, was taken to a room where Weinstein waited for her alone. There, he sexually assaulted her. It was only afterward that she met with the female casting executive. "Everything was designed to make me feel comfortable before it happened," Evans said.[5]

In their phones, Weinstein's assistants filed the women he preyed on as "FOH," or "Friend of Harvey," and compiled "bibles" of advice for their successors on how to arrange such encounters. They even procured Weinstein's erectile dysfunction medication and made sure he had it before "meetings" with young women.[6] Later, some of these assistants claimed to feel remorse for contributing to a "culture of silence about sexual assault" in their company and the entertainment industry at large. Yet they facilitated Weinstein's crimes for years.[7]

In 2015, TWC employee Lauren O'Connor sent an explosive memo to high-level executives alleging that Weinstein had enlisted her and others to arrange liaisons with "vulnerable women who hope he will get them work."[8] The memo made its way to TWC's board of directors—a board Harvey and his business-partner brother, Bob, had packed with loyalists. One of the few board members not appointed by the Weinsteins, Lance Maerov, reportedly demanded that an outside lawyer investigate O'Connor's accusations. But within days, Weinstein negotiated a settlement, O'Connor withdrew her complaint, and the investigation was called off. Board members, including Bob Weinstein, briefly considered refusing to renew Harvey Weinstein's employment contract but ultimately abandoned the idea.

Higher-level employees enabled Weinstein's behavior as well. The head of Miramax Italy, Fabrizio Lombardo, invited Italian-born actor Asia Argento to a party but instead delivered her to Weinstein's hotel room, where the producer sexually

assaulted her. Lombardo was widely known as "Weinstein's pimp in Europe," several sources told Farrow.[9] Another Weinstein complicitor, former Miramax marketing chief Dennis Rice, reported that company funds were available "in the event that there was an indiscretion that needed to be taken care of," such as "bullying, physical abuse, sexual harassment."[10] Between 1990 and 2015, Weinstein reached at least eight financial settlements with women he was accused of harassing, typically in exchange for keeping quiet, Kantor and Twohey reported in the *New York Times*.[11] And there's little doubt that Miramax lawyer-complicitor Steve Hutensky, known by some in the firm as "the Cleaner-Upper," according to Farrow, knew the magnitude of his boss's indiscretions and crimes.[12]

The circle of complicity went well beyond Weinstein's employees. While Weinstein's low-level assistants escorted his prey to and from hotel rooms, a myriad of Hollywood agents and managers *arranged* the meetings, then advised their clients to keep quiet once they learned what Weinstein had done to them. Actor Gwyneth Paltrow's agent at CAA (a top talent agency) set up a hotel room meeting between Paltrow and the man Paltrow knew as "Uncle Harvey," then failed to take action when Paltrow reported that she'd had to dodge his advances. At least eight other CAA agents knew about Weinstein's behavior but didn't act on it. Why? "For agents, actors might come and go, but Mr. Weinstein was one of Hollywood's seemingly permanent fixtures, distributing as many as 30 films a year," the *Times* noted.[13] Weinstein's films earned more than three hundred Academy Award nominations and, according to Farrow in the *New Yorker*, he was thanked more than nearly anyone else in film history at awards ceremonies, "ranking just after Steven Spielberg and right before God."[14] In fact, in her 2012 Golden Globe acceptance speech for her role in *The Iron Lady*,

a Weinstein film, actor Meryl Streep jokingly referred to the producer as "God."

Actor Mira Sorvino, who narrowly escaped being trapped alone with Weinstein twice, believes she was blacklisted after telling a female Miramax employee that she was afraid of the producer. Sorvino concluded, "When people go up against power brokers, there is punishment."[15] Director Peter Jackson revealed that Miramax had warned him not to hire Sorvino and actor Ashley Judd—who had also fended off Weinstein in a hotel room—for *The Lord of the Rings* in the late 1990s because they were "a nightmare to work with." Only in hindsight did Jackson recognize that "this was very likely the Miramax smear campaign in full swing."[16]

Politically motivated complicitors existed on both sides of the aisle. Weinstein was a prominent Democratic Party donor and prolific fundraiser, and many Democratic politicians, including Hillary Clinton, chose to ignore the rumors and allegations against him. And in 2017, former New York governor Republican George Pataki, whose campaign Weinstein had contributed to, tipped off Weinstein that NBC reporter Ronan Farrow was working on a story exposing the many allegations of abuse against him—an exposé Weinstein thought he'd been successful in getting called off.[17] In response, Weinstein threatened NBC executives that he'd go public with accusations of sexual improprieties by Matt Lauer, cohost of NBC's *Today* show. Hillary Clinton's publicist, Nick Merrill, pressured Farrow to abandon his reporting on Weinstein, warning that the "big story" he was working on was a "*concern* for us."[18] NBC ordered Farrow to drop the story entirely. The politicians and network executives who worked to suppress the Weinstein story were complicit in perpetuating the producer's crimes, while the *New Yorker*, the magazine that ultimately published

Farrow's story, can take pride in avoiding complicity and stopping him from harming others.

The Weinstein story landed on Hollywood like a bomb in the fall of 2017, forcing the entertainment industry to acknowledge and address its code of silence. After Weinstein was convicted in February 2020, actor Rose McGowan told Farrow that she felt as if she could finally exhale. But she was left wondering about the "good people"—those who were complicit in helping "sick" Weinstein commit his crimes. "My problem was always with the rest of them who aren't supposedly sick," she said. "What's wrong with them?"[19]

Deference to Authority

The allegations against Harvey Weinstein set off a tidal wave of sexual assault and harassment accusations against prominent men in virtually every realm, fueling the "Me Too" movement. The resulting press exposed dozens of abusive authority figures, among them NBC's Matt Lauer, TV host Charlie Rose, CBS chairperson and CEO Les Moonves, actor Kevin Spacey, singer R. Kelly, and chef Mario Batali, and added credence to accusers' claims that had been shrugged off or ignored for years against luminaries such as Woody Allen, Bill Cosby, Michael Jackson, and Dominique Strauss-Kahn, the former head of the International Monetary Fund. None of these men would have been able to harass, assault, or rape for as long as they did without complicitors.

In his book *The Righteous Mind*, psychologist Jonathan Haidt argues that people vary in how they define ethical behavior.[20] While some think about ethics as involving concern for others and fairness, others view deference to authority as a foundation of ethical behavior. These individuals tend to put greater value on trusting existing institutions and tradition. We will return

to Haidt's discussion of different moral foundations of moral behavior later in the chapter.

I accept that many people likely value tradition and authority more than I do. And I fully appreciate that many people find themselves without the resources required to stand up to authority. But anytime we act against others' well-being by failing to speak up about harm perpetrated by an authority, we need to recognize *at a minimum* that we are making an ethical choice. Silence is an action. Blindly deferring to authority can lead to complicity. This applies far beyond the domain of sexual assault to contexts where authority figures are involved in wrongdoing, including deception, price fixing, illegal kickbacks, fraud, stock-price manipulation, and more.

My views about the dangers of deferring to authority are far from unique. We've all heard the phrase "I was only following orders," which was a common defense offered by high-level Nazis during the Nuremberg trials at the end of World War II.[21] Many Nazis claimed that they should be found innocent because they were simply carrying out the directives of a higher-level authority figure. In response, one of the principles that emerged from the Nuremberg trials, Principle IV, limits deference to authority as an ethical excuse for committing war crimes: "The fact that a person acted pursuant to order of his Government or of a superior does not relieve him from responsibility under international law, provided a moral choice was in fact possible to him."[22]

Loyalty and Institutional Complicity

Harvey Weinstein was an authority figure who sexually assaulted less powerful people. Other egregious stories of complicity with sexual assault come from the worlds of academia, sports, and religion. In these cases, loyalty to an institution often appeared

to be a dominant motivator of complicity. For example, in September 2016 the *Indianapolis Star* reported that two women had filed lawsuits against Dr. Larry Nassar, an osteopath who treated female gymnasts as an employee of USA Gymnastics (USAG) and Michigan State University (MSU), alleging that he sexually abused them under the guise of treating them.[23] After the story broke, many other women came forward with similar allegations. Nassar was arrested in December 2016 on child pornography charges, pleaded guilty, and was sentenced to 60 years in federal prison, as well as 40 to 125 more years in Michigan for three counts of sexual assault. On January 13, 2018, a Michigan judge said there were "over 265 identified victims and an infinite number of victims [of Nassar's] in the state, in the country, and all over the world."[24]

At MSU, many trainers, coaches, and officials, including university president Lou Anna Simon, were informed of Nassar's predation over a twenty-year period. Every one of these complicitors failed to act. In fact, even after Nassar was under investigation, MSU allowed him to see patients for another sixteen months. In 2018, MSU settled lawsuits filed by 332 accusers of Nassar for $500 million.[25] USAG and U.S. Olympic Committee officials also failed to address a stream of allegations of sexual abuse against Nassar and others.[26] In January 2018, the entire governing board of USAG resigned under pressure, and the organization filed for bankruptcy by the end of the year.

In a January 2018 ESPN article entitled "Nassar Surrounded by Adults Who Enabled His Predatory Behavior," John Barr and Dan Murphy write,

> Understanding how Nassar gained unfettered access to young girls and young women over the course of a quarter-century—despite repeated warning signs—means confronting

an uncomfortable truth: He didn't gain that access alone. Nassar was surrounded by a collection of adults who enabled his predatory behavior—a group that included coaches of club, collegiate and elite-level gymnasts, the USA Gymnastics organization, medical professionals, administrators and coaches at Michigan State University, and gymnasts' parents, whom he groomed just as effectively as those he violated.[27]

In July 2019, an eighteen-month congressional investigation concluded that the U.S. Olympic Committee and USAG "knowingly concealed" Nassar's abuse and that the FBI had failed to seriously consider the allegations.[28] Many adults deferred to Nassar's authority as a physician, taking his word over the accusations of children and young women. In addition, many coaches and trainers who were close to Nassar prioritized loyalty to him over protecting children. Similarly, leaders at MSU, USAG, and the U.S. Olympic Committee showed blind loyalty to their institutions at the expense of young people's safety. It took until late 2021 for USAG and the U.S. Olympic and Paralympic Committee to agree to pay $380 million to settle a lawsuit filed by more than five hundred survivors of sexual abuse by Larry Nassar.[29]

Even FBI agents charged with protecting victims showed a strange deference to Nassar. Just two weeks before the 2021 Tokyo Olympics, the Justice Department's inspector general released a report concluding that the FBI had failed to properly investigate Nassar, dismissing reports from victims. FBI officials then tried to cover up their complicity when confronted about their failures. Olympian McKayla Maroney told the Senate Judiciary Committee in September 2021 that in 2015, she reported Nassar's repeated abuse of her to an FBI

agent, Michael Langeman, even before she had told her mother what had happened. After Maroney spent three hours detailing the abuse to him, she says, Langeman responded, "Is that all?" The FBI failed to report Maroney's accusations for seventeen months, then "made entirely false claims about what I said," she testified. "They chose to lie about what I said and protect a serial child molester rather than protect not only me but countless others."[30] The FBI's botched response allowed Nassar to abuse at least seventy more women and girls before Michigan officials finally arrested him. Numerous senators on the committee expressed outrage that the Department of Justice had not filed criminal charges against FBI agents and sports and government officials who failed to act to stop Nassar. "A whole lot of people should be in prison," Senator Patrick Leahy concluded.[31]

On June 22, 2012, Jerry Sandusky, a former football coach at Penn State, was convicted on forty-five counts of sexually abusing eight boys under the age of thirteen between 1994 and 2009. Sandusky gained access to his victims through his leadership of a charity serving underprivileged youth, often involving them in the Penn State football program. Multiple Penn State employees witnessed Sandusky's abuse, and many high-level officials, including famed head football coach Joe Paterno and university president Graham Spanier, learned about the abuse and failed to report it to the police, as required by law. In 2021, Spanier was sentenced to two months in prison for his role as a complicitor in Sandusky's crimes. The overwhelming theme across the complicitors was loyalty to Penn State, specifically Penn State football.

The most extensive group of sexual predators and complicitors in modern history were members of the religious hierarchy of the Catholic Church. Beginning in the late 1980s, news

stories began to emerge worldwide of priests who had habitually abused young parishioners. Across countries, cultures, and
even centuries, the hierarchy of the Catholic Church failed to
act on massive evidence of abuse by priests. During the twentieth century, church leadership habitually transferred priests
who were accused of sexual abuse to other parishes with the
intent of keeping their crimes under wraps. Inevitably, these
priests continued to abuse children as they were shuffled from
church to church.

One striking exemplar was Cardinal Bernard F. Law, the
archbishop of Boston, whose failure to act on accusations of
child abuse against dozens of priests in his jurisdiction over
nearly two decades allowed hundreds of additional parishioners to be raped. Cardinal Law knew about molestation
accusations against John J. Geoghan yet returned the priest to
parish work after he received treatment for pedophilia. Over
the course of thirty years, Geoghan was accused of sexually
abusing 130 boys at six parishes; he was imprisoned in 2002.
Law, a former civil rights activist, knowingly kept numerous
criminals active in the priesthood and violated many laws
along the way.[32] In 2004, Pope John Paul II appointed Law
to a post in Rome, which granted him Vatican citizenship and
enabled him to avoid possible criminal prosecution; Law died
in 2017.

In all of these stories of institutional complicity with evil,
leaders who were responsible for protecting children allowed
men to repeatedly abuse them. Many of the more senior complicitors, including the presidents of MSU and Penn State,
Paterno, and Law, were not deferring to a predator's authority but rather were loyal to the institution in which the sexual
assaults took place. Research on loyalty can help us better
understand how it can lead to complicity with evil, particularly

when it is perpetuated by the powerful—and how we ourselves can avoid this trap.

The Pros and Cons of Loyalty

Harvard philosopher and psychologist Joshua Greene writes about the many ways in which humans give favorable treatment to members of their own "tribe," with tribe being defined as a subgroup of the general population to which an individual feels an emotional attachment.[33] Tribes can be families, religions, nations, or organizations. One small tribe that many of us join is called a marriage. In the context of this tribe, Greene highlights the power and benefit of loyalty. Imagine that you are twenty-six years old and marry someone the same age. Your mutual decision to marry conveys that each of you feels that the other tribe member's kindness, physical attractiveness, humor, wealth, income-earning potential, and other factors that may be important to you are sufficiently high that you are willing to forgo other matching opportunities that may come along before you're settled into middle age (at least, that's the commitment you make at your wedding). Notice, each of you has met only a minority of the many matching partners you might meet in the years ahead. What motivates you to form a stable marriage, one where the dogs and kids can more or less depend on both of you to stick around full-time? (Of course, marriage isn't an enforceable guarantee; divorce is common.) One obvious force that binds the two of you is love, which prompts a romantic version of loyalty. As a result of this loyalty, each of you explicitly or implicitly agrees to value the other party to such a degree that you no longer regularly assess your alternatives or weigh the costs and benefits of the current match, Greene notes.

Of course, we are loyal to many people in life, aside from any lifetime romantic partner. Many definitions of loyalty mention constructs like devotion and faithfulness. For the purposes of this chapter, I define loyalty as a commitment to act in the interests of another person, other people, or an organization without deliberating about whether such actions are rational or ethically optimal. In this process, loyalty becomes a basis for System 1 decision-making and eliminates more systematic thought.

Many organizations and leaders expect or demand loyalty from their members. Military and religious organizations are particularly focused on member loyalty. Supporters of sports teams and political candidates are also often loyal, even to the point that they are unable to see obvious limitations in their preferred team, athlete, or politician. Psychologists refer to our inability to see the bad in people and organizations to whom we are loyal as an aspect of motivated blindness.[34] When those to whom we are loyal commit evil acts, we are at risk of ignoring their crimes or dismissing them as untrue—and becoming complicit.

My own general lack of loyalty may prevent me from fully empathizing with people who tend to be more loyal than I am. I am loyal to my spouse, my dog, and many of my former doctoral students, but when my favorite sports team (the Pittsburgh Steelers) hired a convicted animal abuser as their backup quarterback, I stopped being a fan. And when evidence suggested that the New England Patriots' star quarterback, Tom Brady, was a cheater, and that his cheating was enabled by the team's head coach, Bill Belichick, and owner, Robert Kraft, I couldn't emotionally empathize with my generally ethical colleagues and friends who were in denial about the evidence. Of course, complicity in the form of rooting for your local sports

team is not in the same league as the complicity with sexual predators discussed earlier. Rather, I offer this less important story to highlight how easy it is to see the effects of loyalty in our own behavior.

I trust that the dark side of loyalty is now obvious, as documented in the complicity with evil that otherwise ethical people at MSU, Penn State, the Catholic Church, and other institutions have demonstrated. Being loyal to the point of suppressing deliberation can lead individuals to support evildoers and their organizations, even when profound harm is being done to others. In these cases, loyalty moves from a virtue to an evil. Legal scholar Amos Guiora has written two books on complicity. The first, *The Crime of Complicity: The Bystander in the Holocaust*,[35] was motivated by his experience as the child of Holocaust survivors. In his more recent book, *Armies of Enablers*, he interviews survivors of sexual assaults that were facilitated by churches, universities, and other institutions, including the Catholic Church, MSU, and Penn State.[36] In their own words, the survivors reveal that, over and above the physical and psychological harm their perpetrators inflicted on them, they also have felt psychologically abused by complicitors' failure to stop the criminals. For many of the survivors Guiora interviews, this loyalty of the complicit to their institution violated the trust that survivors had in that same institution.

Loyalty describes the best and worst of our behaviors. It conjures up images of heroism on the battlefield, sacrifices for family members and friends, and the enduring commitments we make to our work, regardless of the cost. But loyalty is also evident when people betray their nation in support of their subgroup, support criminals, and keep quiet while members of their group break the law. Thus, loyalty can serve to bind members of a group or an organization but also lead them to

engage in corruption, cheating, and abuse. Research clarifies that people are most likely to cheat to help other group members when their group is in competition with other groups.[37] This may explain why we so often see the downside of loyalty in sports, in the form of gamesmanship and cheating scandals in support of one's team.

Loyalty often leads us to favoritism, or the practice of treating members of our group more generously than we would treat outsiders. It can also mean not acting to stop the unethical behavior of those to whom we are loyal. When we allow members of our group to engage in evil behavior that imposes larger costs on society, we are complicit in their wrongdoing.

Loyalty to the Corporation

Legal scholars Adi Libson and Gideon Parchomovsky offer a careful look at the downsides of loyalty within corporations. After highlighting the well-known advantages of having loyal employees, they argue that "loyalty, like the God Janus, has two faces. While almost all theorists have focused on the bright side of loyalty . . . we show that loyalty can be the bane of corporations."[38] They then document the profound costs of loyalty in three major recent corporate scandals—at Boeing, General Motors, and Volkswagen, the last of which we encountered in chapter 3.

On November 28, 2018, a Lion Air flight crashed into the ocean right after taking off in Indonesia, killing all 189 people on board. On March 10, 2019, an Ethiopian Airlines jet crashed in similar form, just after takeoff, killing all 157 people on board. In each crash, the plane was one of Boeing's new 737 Max aircrafts. Three days after the Ethiopian Airlines disaster, the U.S. Federal Aviation Administration (FAA) grounded the remaining 737 Maxes. U.S. regulators fined Boeing over $2.5 billion for

its role in the two crashes after the U.S. Department of Justice concluded that Boeing's failure resulted, to a significant degree, from its rush to bring its new airplane to market with inadequate testing amid its sales competition with Airbus. Libson and Parchomovsky focus on the role of Mark Forkner, the chief technical pilot involved in the testing of the 737 Max. During the testing, Forkner identified problems that, if discovered by the FAA, would have slowed down the launch of the new design. "So I basically lied to the regulators (unknowingly)," he later said.[39] A congressional investigation found that his emails and text messages were part of a broader pattern at Boeing that emphasized profits over safety. Why would Forkner hide his concerns from the FAA? Loyalty to his employer appears to have implicitly affected his actions.

On February 6, 2014, General Motors (GM) started a recall process that would eventually involve nearly thirty million cars. Faulty ignition switches were causing the engines of some GM vehicles to shut down while in motion, while also keeping airbags from inflating.[40] GM would eventually pay settlements to the families of 124 people who died as a result of this problem and $900 million in penalties to the U.S. government. Shockingly, GM had known about the faulty switch for at least a decade prior to the recall.[41]

At the heart of the scandal was Raymond DeGiorgio, a GM engineer who was asked to choose a nice-looking switch that would upgrade the image of the company's small cars.[42] When the switch he chose in 2001, made by supplier Delphi, began failing, DeGiorgio tried to have it replaced with a newer part, but a high-level GM product committee rejected his request. In violation of company policy, DeGiorgio secretly ordered a modified switch from Delphi, a move that fixed the problem for newer GM vehicles but didn't address the risk to cars already on

the road. After it was implicated in the crisis, GM fired DeGiorgio, blaming him for approving the substandard switch in the first place. DeGiorgio viewed himself as "nothing more than a loyal worker whose best efforts got him fired and made him a target of possible criminal charges," according to the *New York Times*.[43] Numerous GM employees told the *Times* that the company's culture, in which thousands of mid-level engineers stagnate with little oversight, was responsible for the crisis. "All I can say is that I did my job," DeGiorgio told the *Times*. "I didn't lie, cheat or steal. I did my job the best I could."[44] By creating incentives for DeGiorgio to stay quiet and failing to properly monitor of his work, senior management at GM became complicit in the deaths caused by the ignition switch. DeGiorgio was complicit, too, as his loyalty to the organization played a significant role in the death of the company's customers.

Libson and Parchomovsky's account of the Dieselgate scandal at Volkswagen also focuses on a specific automotive engineer, James Robert Liang. In 2016, Liang pleaded guilty for his role in a nearly ten-year conspiracy at Volkswagen to deceive customers by designing software to cheat U.S. emissions tests. Liang admitted that when he and his fellow engineers were unable to design a diesel engine that would meet U.S. emissions standards, they developed software that would deceive U.S. emissions tests instead. Liang argued that he was just following orders; his lawyer, Daniel Nixon, characterized Liang as having "blindly executed a misguided loyalty to his employer."[45] The U.S. District Court judge trying his case appeared to agree, saying Liang was "too loyal" to the German automaker he had worked for since the 1980s.[46] Liang was sentenced to forty months in federal prison for his role in the conspiracy.

Loyalty to their employers appeared to motivate Forkner, DeGiorgio, and Liang to engage in behaviors that made them

complicit in devastating corporate crises. Why might loyalty drive people to sacrifice nearly everything, from their ethics to their personal freedom to the lives of others? In his landmark 1975 book *Sociobiology*, biologist E. O. Wilson points to loyalty's evolutionary roots.[47] In early human tribes, members gained a better chance of procreating by cooperating with their tribe, though they may have needed to work against their more myopically defined self-interest to do so, writes Wilson.[48] While loyal members make personal sacrifices on the tribe's behalf, as a whole, all tribe members benefit from their actions. Notably, cooperative tribes are more likely to reproduce and survive than less cooperative tribes. Thus, loyalty may improve a group's biological fitness and could help to explain why we continue to engage in destructive behaviors that we think will benefit our group. But helping our group survive does not make a behavior moral or legal—and it could make us complicit in its wrongdoing.

Individuals' decisions about which groups they choose to reward with their loyalty can also affect their complicity. Philosopher Peter Singer argues that we reach the most ethical decisions when we make the group to which we belong as large as possible.[49] Singer's version of utilitarianism argues for treating everyone's interests equally, leaving no room for valuing members of your group over other people or even other species. Most of us are unwilling and unable to value people on the other side of the planet to the same degree as our own family members. But by enlarging our sphere of concern, we tend to be more ethical and create more value in the world, Singer argues. Sociobiology may have moved us in the direction of smaller clans, such as our extended family. Yet, Singer notes, our cognitive evolution gives us the power to ethically move beyond caring for only a small group and enlarge our circle.[50]

Most of us can understand blind loyalty to one's close family. But why would we show extreme loyalty to employers, especially in our era of layoffs and huge pay gaps between CEOs and average workers? Part of the answer is that organizations with more loyal employees may well be at a competitive advantage when it comes to surviving in the market. And organizations, more than families, churches, or neighborhood associations, can select members based on loyalty and fire those they deem less loyal. Thus, loyalty may be rewarded, even to the point of shifting employees toward having blind faith in the corporate mission. When a conflict arises between the interests of the organization and those of society at large, the loyal employee doesn't pause to consider what the ethical action would be. Instead, relying on System 1 loyalty, they commit or go along with unethical acts on behalf of the organization.

The Blue Wall of Silence

Minneapolis police officer Derek Chauvin's murder of George Floyd in broad daylight on May 25, 2020, caught on video, was a horrifying crime that galvanized a movement to end police brutality. Three other Minneapolis officers—J. Alexander Kueng, Thomas Lane, and Tou Thao—watched Chauvin kill the unarmed man and did nothing to stop him. On February 24, 2022, Kueng, Lane, and Thao were found guilty of federal crimes of violating Floyd's civil rights by failing to intervene while Chauvin killed him; the three also face a Minnesota state trial.[51] What is unusual about Chauvin's murder is not that other officers were loyal to Chauvin but that they are being held accountable for their apparent crimes.

In the United States, the term "blue wall of silence" refers to the informal but deep-seated code of silence that leads police

to be loyal to their fellow officers to the extent that they fail to act on or report colleagues' mistakes, misconduct, and crimes, including brutality. Despite being illegal and informal, the blue wall is systemic and institutionalized.

In May 2021, the Associated Press (AP) published previously unreleased body-camera footage from May 10, 2019, of white Louisiana State Police troopers stunning, beating, and dragging an unarmed Black man named Ronald Greene at the end of a high-speed chase. The troopers left Greene prone and shackled facedown for more than nine minutes as he apologized for the chase and begged for mercy. Six troopers were on the scene. An emergency room doctor wrote in a medical report that Greene arrived dead at the hospital, bruised, bloodied, and with two stun-gun prongs in his back. "Does not add up," the doctor wrote of troopers' claim that Greene had died upon crashing into a tree.[52] Nonetheless, the Union Parish coroner classified Greene's death as accidental and caused by cardiac arrest.

One of the troopers involved in the incident, Chris Hollingsworth, bragged to a colleague back at the office that he had "beat the ever-living f—out of" Greene, "choked him and everything else trying to get him under control," until Greene "was spitting blood . . . and all of a sudden he just went limp."[53] The State Police later admitted that Greene died on his way to the hospital, but fifteen months passed before the department, under growing pressure from Greene's family, politicians, and the media, opened an investigation into the attack. Refusing to release the video of the incident, the State Police claimed the troopers' use of force was justified. While Hollingsworth was eventually fired, the other five troopers present were not.

A subsequent AP investigation uncovered at least a dozen cases in the prior decade in which Louisiana State Police troopers or their superiors ignored or covered up evidence

of beatings of crime suspects.[54] Troopers routinely turned off or muted their body cameras while pursuing suspects, the AP found. When footage was recorded, the police agency typically refused to release it, did not review it, and lost or ignored it in a "digital vault."[55] Troopers also sometimes omitted uses of force, including head blows, from official police reports, in addition to falsely portraying suspects as aggressive. Most of those beaten were Black.

"Even as bad cops evade punishment for wrongdoing, those who stand up to corruption, report negligence or abuse, or decline to comply with bad orders are frequently marginalized, demoted, or outright fired," writes Columbia University sociology fellow Musa al-Gharbi in the *Atlantic*.[56] Al-Gharbi recounts the case of Buffalo Police Department officer Cariol Horne, who arrived at a crime scene to find a fellow officer, Gregory Kwiatkowski, choking a handcuffed Black man while other officers watched. Horne pleaded with Kwiatkowski not to kill the man. When he ignored her, she pulled his arm from around the suspect's neck. Enraged, Kwiatkowski punched Horne in the face. Rather than punishing him for assaulting another officer, the Buffalo police fired Horne for obstructing justice.[57] Kwiatkowski went on to choke another officer on the job, attack another officer while off duty, and use brutal force against four handcuffed Black teens. He pleaded guilty to using excessive force in this later instance and in other arrests. He was sentenced to only four months in jail and, unlike Horne, was allowed to retire from the force and keep his pension.

"The system protects cops like [Derek] Chauvin, who had at least 17 previous misconduct complaints and had been involved in multiple incidents in which he or another officer used lethal force," al-Gharbi concludes, while officers who try to stop others from engaging in brutality or speak up about it are often

punished severely or fired. "This is perhaps one of the most significant yet largely neglected problems with policing in America: Departments are making an example not of the so-called bad apples, but of the good ones."[58]

A 2021 study by researchers at the University of Washington published in the *Lancet*, a major medical journal, suggests a broad network of complicity in covering up police violence.[59] Comparing information from the National Vital Statistics System, which collects death certificates, with data from organizations that track police killings through news reports and public records requests, the researchers found that medical examiners listed about 17,000 of nearly 31,000 fatal encounters with the police between 1980 and 2018, or 55 percent of these fatalities, as another cause of death, such as cardiac arrest. In some cases, medical examiners failed to investigate law enforcement's involvement in the death or to mention it on the death certificate, as was true for Ronald Greene's death; other deaths were incorrectly coded in a national database. In the case of George Floyd, backing up the police's claims that drug use and underlying health conditions had contributed to his death, a Hennepin County medical examiner attributed it to "cardiopulmonary arrest" despite the fact that bystander video clearly showed Floyd being asphyxiated by a police officer. The medical examination system "has long been criticized for fostering a cozy relationship with law enforcement—forensic pathologists regularly consult with detectives and prosecutors and in some jurisdictions they are directly employed by police agencies," according to the *New York Times*.[60] Other officers, superiors, and medical examiners have frequently been complicit in hiding the true amount of violence committed by police officers. In addition, when our elected officials fail to reform the police system, they join the ranks of the complicit.

Explaining Our Deference to Authority and Loyalty

Earlier in the chapter, I mentioned psychologist Jonathan Haidt's argument that people differ in their views of what constitutes moral behavior. His book argues more specifically that people differ in their views of morality based on the weight they attach to six core moral foundations: care, fairness (or justice), respect for authority, loyalty, sanctity (or purity), and liberty.[61] He defines them as follows:

- The Care foundation views morality in terms of kindness, nurturing, and protecting and understanding the distress or suffering of those in need.
- The Fairness foundation views morality in terms of rights and justice. While fairness advocates define fairness differently (for example, whether it should be based on equality or proportionality), the overall focus is determining what is fair.
- The Loyalty foundation views morality in terms of a willingness to sacrifice for the good of the group and patriotism.
- The Authority foundation views morality in terms of valuing leadership, deference, and tradition.
- The Sanctity foundation views morality in terms of purity and sanctity. This foundation often operates on the view that, unlike non-human animals, people have souls.
- The Liberty foundation views morality in terms of the value of freedom and our right to it. This foundation focuses on individual rights and is against the state imposing its will on its citizens.

Haidt provides evidence that the current political polarization in the United States and other countries can be attributed

to the left and the right defining morality differently, in predictable ways. The left tends to focus on care and fairness exclusively, while the right also focuses on authority, loyalty, purity, and liberty. Haidt's work is very controversial; many of his left-leaning colleagues in the social sciences think his recognition of the latter four foundations amounts to an endorsement of unethical behavior that they do not view as part of the moral equation. They reject the idea that it is justifiable to ignore justice and caring for others based on loyalty, authority, sanctity, and liberty concerns. Haidt argues that the political left will lose elections if it limits arguments to just two moral foundations that do not encompass the views of the majority of the electorate.

I personally think that concern for other human beings (and other species) and for fairness should lead us to recognize situations in which being loyal, obedient, pure, or independent leads to unethical decisions—particularly given my preference for maximizing value for all. I don't support loyalty that is undeserved or obedience to evil leaders. Throughout this chapter, I have documented numerous episodes where I think that complicitors should have overridden their loyalty and deference to authority based on concerns for justice and care for others. Nevertheless, I appreciate how Haidt's framework helps us understand differences in how people think about moral behavior. If we are using different foundations to define morality, we will categorize different behaviors as moral and immoral.

Haidt's framework also helps me understand the behavior of people who defer to powerful harm doers, even if I disagree with their choices. Moreover, beyond political affiliation, Haidt's moral foundations help to explain the role we play in our organizations. It becomes easier to see how those in power (including religious, business, and family leaders) might select

for and reward loyal behavior. Once people start viewing loyalty as ethical, and it becomes a System 1 response, they may fail to speak up when evil is being done in their organizations, particularly by those in power. They may even help to perpetuate it. When group members put their unquestioning faith in the powerful, they will not have the reason needed to avoid complicity in their actions.

7

Trust in Our Relationships

In the summer of 2021, when I was nearly finished with the first draft of this book, three respected social science researchers—Uri Simonsohn, Joe Simmons, and Leif Nelson—published a post on the academic blog DataColada (http://datacolada.org /98) entitled "Evidence of Fraud in an Influential Field Experiment about Dishonesty."[1] The authors presented compelling evidence that the well-cited research paper "Signing at the Beginning Makes Ethics Salient and Decreases Dishonest Self-Reports in Comparison to Signing at the End" was fraudulent. Unfortunately, I was a coauthor of the paper. While I did not commit the fraud, I was complicit in the fraud that was uncovered. My trust in others was central to my complicity.

This chapter documents my struggle in this story to manage the many benefits of being trusting against the risk of becoming a complicitor. As I will document, I was far from a passive observer. When I saw possible ethical problems with data, I did seek clarification. But I too readily accepted the answers I was given when I should have pushed even harder. This failure to push harder created my complicity.

Lisa Shu, Nina Mazar, Francesca Gino, Dan Ariely, and I published the paper in question in 2012 in the journal *Proceedings of the National Academy of Sciences* (*PNAS*).[2] The paper aimed to identify a simple intervention that "nudges" people to be more honest when filling out forms, such as their income tax return or a mileage report for the company that insures their car. Specifically, based on the results of three experiments, we claimed that if an organization asks people to sign a statement promising to tell the truth *before* they fill out a form, they will provide more honest information than if they sign such a statement *after* providing the requested information. We predicted that reminding people up front of their obligation to be truthful would prompt them to respond more honestly. And, indeed, this is what our experiments all appeared to show.

The paper combined two previously unpublished empirical efforts: (1) two laboratory experiments by Shu, Gino, and me that claimed to demonstrate the "signing first" effect, and (2) one field experiment conducted at an insurance company, previously described by Ariely in multiple public forums. Gino initiated the contact to Ariely, who responded positively to the idea of joining together and added, "I have been working on this with Nina—so this will have to involve her as well." In 2021, after the scandal broke, Mazar clarified that her prior collaboration with Ariely on the topic was limited to mentioning the idea of "signing first" in a prior publication of theirs and said they were not actively working on the topic prior to contact from Gino. Gino contacted Mazar, who also agreed to join, writing that "it's a good idea to combine forces." By early 2011, the five of us had combined efforts, realizing that the two projects responded to limitations of the other: the Shu-Gino-Bazerman studies claimed to offer well-controlled laboratory

experiments, while the field study claimed to provide an experiment using data from an insurance company.

In the field experiment, customers were said to have signed an honesty statement either before or after reporting mileage from their car's odometer. Because the insurance company would charge customers more if they drove more, customers had a monetary incentive to (unethically) underreport their mileage. Data were ostensibly collected from customers twice; each customer had provided their odometer reading earlier, before the researchers were involved, and a second time, after the researchers assigned them to one of two conditions (signing the honesty statement *before* reporting mileage or signing *after* reporting mileage). The key measure in the field experiment was the difference between the two mileage reports, which would provide a measure of how many miles customers drove during that period of time. It was important for customers to be randomly assigned to one of the two conditions, as this would ensure that any difference observed in mileage reporting could be causally explained by whether they signed before or after reporting their mileage a second time. The field experiment was represented as involving randomly assigning customers to one of the two conditions.

In February 2011, all authors received a draft of the new, combined paper. Gino, Shu, and Mazar had worked on it before I saw a draft. This was the first opportunity I'd had to examine the insurance-company study in any detail. The write-up of that experiment claimed that customers who signed the honesty statement *after* reporting their odometer mileage had driven 23,601 miles in the past year and that customers who signed the honesty statement *before* reporting their mileage had driven 26,098 miles in the past year—2,427 more miles than those who signed the honesty statement after. This was a very large,

statistically significant difference. The implication was that when signing on the front end of a form, people considered the ethical dimension of what they were about to report, which made them less likely to lie by underreporting their mileage.

The data in the insurance experiment made me nervous. Specifically, I found it strange that people had driven such a large number of miles in one year in both conditions—averaging over 24,000 miles. "The means for the number of miles driven in a year seem enormous—twice what I would have expected," I wrote to my coauthors in March 2011. "Am I simply wrong, is the sample unusual, or is there an error in recording the data?" Ariely responded to me quickly with a brief email: "The milage [sic] are correct." Over the next few weeks, I had multiple discussions in person with Shu and Gino at Harvard in which I communicated my suspicions about the data—specifically, the number of miles driven, which seemed to me to be abnormally high.

My concerns led to further communication among the five authors. In an April 2011 email, Ariely provided more information about the source of the data: "We used an older population mostly in Florida—but we can't tell how we got the data, who was the population (they were all AARP members)—and we also can't show the forms . . ." I still did not understand why the customers' mileage would be so high and received no good answers to my questions throughout the rest of 2011.

In January 2012, I attended a professional conference in San Diego, where I ran into Lisa Shu, who was my advisee, a coauthor of mine on other papers, and a friend. Shu was with Nina Mazar, whom I had never met. After Shu introduced us, I expressed my significant concern about Ariely's lack of clarity in explaining the mileage issue I had questioned. I told Shu and Mazar that I didn't think Ariely's explanation—that the data came from an elderly population—accounted for what seemed

to me to be abnormally high mileage numbers. Mazar pulled out her laptop and found the data file that we were discussing. She said that while Ariely may not have explained the issue well enough, we were simply dealing with a minor issue regarding how to explain the data. As I recall that conversation, Mazar said she believed that the confusion came from the first odometer reading, which customers provided before being assigned to a sign-before or sign-after condition. Specifically, she explained that it wasn't clear when the first readings had been taken, and it may have been more than a year before the second readings were taken. Thus, the first draft of the write-up of the study apparently was not accurate in stating that there had been a year between the two mileage reports. The implication was that the time difference between the mileage reporting was unclear, rather than that the mileage data were wrong. Mazar's explanation was plausible and consistent with the general trust I have in my coauthors. In the past, I had never considered the possibility that a coauthor had provided fraudulent data. And it didn't occur to me then that the data Mazar received from Ariely and the insurance company might be fraudulent.

I had asked many questions. Thus, the story I am telling of my own complicity is not one of passivity. But it is also important to highlight what I didn't do: I didn't look at the insurance data myself. In fact, as the story unfolded in the media in 2021, I was not even aware that I had ever had direct access to the data, but I had. In 2012, Mazar uploaded a data file to Dropbox and provided access to all five coauthors. I never opened that file; I trusted my coauthors. In 2021, Uri Simonsohn and multiple coauthors[3] of the 2012 paper made me aware that I had access to the file on Dropbox. Had I spent a half hour examining the data, I believe that I could have noticed some of the problems in this story of fraud. This failure to check the data was based

on my trust in my coauthors, a trust that was unwarranted and that made me complicit.

After Ariely communicated further with the insurance company, we changed the description of how the data in the field study was collected, consistent with Mazar's oral report. While I considered Ariely's earlier answers to be inadequate, I wanted to believe the updated explanation and that the study was solid. Lisa Shu was a graduate student at the time, my advisee, and had been presenting this research on the job market as part of her portfolio of ongoing research. I was rooting for her to succeed and wanted this paper to help carry her forward. As I write this book a decade later, I am open to the possibility that I was engaged in motivated blindness.[4]

After we published our paper in 2012, it received a great deal of attention. By the end of 2021, the paper had been cited in other research papers close to five hundred times.[5] Numerous organizations implemented our idea and moved the signature line from the bottom of forms to the top. I believed the core result—that signing first leads to more honest reporting than signing after. I presented our work at universities and when I taught MBA students and executives. In my consulting practice, I advised organizations to move signature lines to the top of forms.

In September 2016, I received an email from Stuart Baserman, the cofounder of Slice Labs, a technology company working to move the insurance industry online (a growing field known as "insurtech"). "A couple of days ago," Baserman wrote, "I was researching the 'psychology of claims' and I came across 'Signing at the beginning makes ethics salient' . . . Of course, the paper and your name caught my attention. If you have some time, it would be nice to learn about you, your work and how it may relate to what we are building at Slice."

I soon met Baserman and began work as a consultant to Slice. (The similarity of our surnames led my spouse to order DNA-testing kits for each of us, which showed that we are very distant cousins.) Part of my consulting assignment involved helping Slice create a platform that would induce claimants to tell the truth online. Working with Slice led me to broaden out from the idea of "signing first" to find ways to induce online honesty, including when people are answering questions and making decisions.

In 2017, I started a research collaboration with Ariella Kristal (then a Harvard PhD student) and Ashley Whillans (then an assistant professor at Harvard) that looked at this broader question of online honesty. Knowing that Slice would be interested in the results of the research, before we began I reached out to Harvard Business School (HBS) officials to confirm that it would be acceptable for me to conduct the basic research using HBS resources, given the relationship between the research and my work for a consulting client—a possible conflict of interest. I received this permission.

Given the apparent success of signing first, documented in the Shu-Mazar-Gino-Ariely-Bazerman 2012 publication, it felt obvious to start by demonstrating the signing-first strategy in an online context. In the Shu-Mazar-Gino-Ariely-Bazerman laboratory studies, participants had shown up at a lab in person, and data was collected using physical forms. I believed that Kristal, Whillans, and I would be conducting an easy extension study that would simply replicate the 2012 results in an online context. Yet our first attempt at replication failed; that is, people's reporting was not statistically different whether they signed before or after filling out an online form. We tried four more times and failed to replicate each time.

We now had five failures to replicate what Shu, Mazar, Gino, Ariely, and I had reported as a large, statistically significant effect in our 2012 paper. Kristal, Whillans, and I decided the next step would be to do a pure replication of one of the laboratory studies from the 2012 paper with a large sample. To be collaborative rather than adversarial, Kristal and Whillans suggested that we invite the other four authors from the original paper (Shu-Mazar-Gino-Ariely) into the project. All four authors agreed to join us. Again we failed to replicate the signing-first effect. The seven of us (Kristal-Whillans-Bazerman-Gino-Shu-Mazar-Ariely) went on to document this failure in a *PNAS* paper in 2020.[6]

In the process of writing this 2020 failure-to-replicate paper, Kristal uncovered an unexplainably large difference in the *first* baseline odometer reading in the field study from the 2012 paper—the mileage that the insurance company's customers reported at least a year before being assigned to the signing-first or signing-after conditions. Namely, there was an enormous difference between the two groups in this first odometer reading, which was taken before any researcher intervened: the baseline mileage for drivers signing *after* mileage reporting was 75,035 miles, while the baseline for drivers signing *first* was 59,693. Researchers call this a "randomization failure," meaning that the two conditions differed on an important outcome before researchers intervened. The likelihood of the two conditions differing by this large amount by chance was less than 1 in 10,000, which raised questions about whether a randomized experiment had even taken place. I expressed this concern to all of my coauthors. In the end, we agreed to document the enormous pre-measure difference in our 2020 publication.

As we worked on the replication project, Kristal, Whillans, and I had regular disagreements with Ariely and Mazar about

the degree to which the new studies invalidated the results published in 2012. Kristal, Whillans, and I favored clearly expressing our view that the signing-first effect did not replicate, while Ariely and Mazar simply wanted to narrow the conclusions of the failure-to-replicate paper. In the interest of reaching a consensus, I made too many concessions. As a result, the 2020 paper is not as critical of our 2012 paper as I argued it should be. I also have no recollection of any of the authors (including me) of the 2020 paper making the argument to initiate the process of retracting the 2012 paper. My failure to fight harder to clearly describe the lack of validity of the 2012 paper made me complicit.

On July 27, 2020, soon after the 2020 paper was published, the editors of *PNAS* asked if our original 2012 paper should be retracted. An email discussion ensued among the five coauthors of the 2012 paper. I was in favor of retraction. On July 28, 2020, Ariely emailed the other four authors, "I am not aware of any experimental error—my guess is that it is just one of these times when the lab produces a different result for some reason— I am not suggesting any mistake . . . I believe that over time the weight of the evidence will be in favor of the first result . . . But—we will see. This is the beautify [*sic*] of this process." A few hours later, Ariely sent another email expressing confidence in the results of the 2012 paper, despite five failures to replicate. Going a step further, he predicted that the *2020 failure-to-replicate* paper would need to be retracted: ". . . I suspect that we will end up retracting the second paper . . . My strong preference is to keep both papers out and let the science process do its job . . ." In an email sent the same day, Mazar wrote, "I do not see reason for retracting our paper given PNAS' criteria. As far as I know we do not have evidence that the findings of our three experiments are unreliable, either as a result of

major error through miscalculation or experimental error . . . From the email thread so far, it looks like the majority agrees that there is no need for retraction. Shall we respond to PNAS with that or is there more need for discussion?"

"It is obvious to me that the original paper was based on unscientific and unethical reporting of data," I wrote the next evening in another email arguing for retraction. "This is the basis of my preference to retract. I think we should all be embarrassed that our names are on the paper—I certainly am embarrassed by having my name on that paper . . . I may be outvoted, but do not read me as being part of a consensus, Max."

Mazar responded to the group within a few hours, requesting that I clarify what was unscientific and unethical about our original data reporting. The next morning, I answered her question: "Reporting a randomized experiment where there was no randomization. Lack of transparency about this issue . . . Obfuscation to multiple questions that I asked in the creation of the original paper . . . Not informing me of the lack of randomization during the creation of the paper." But even then, I did not suspect pure data fabrication in our published work. Shu and I remained the only two authors of the 2012 paper explicitly in favor of retraction. We did not retract the paper in 2020. I think that this was a mistake.

In July 2021, about a year after we passed on the opportunity to retract our 2012 paper, Uri Simonsohn contacted all five of the authors of the 2012 paper to let us know that the DataColada team had drafted a post providing strong evidence that suggested data fraud in the insurance experiment. Mazar quickly proposed that all the paper's authors meet online. I responded that I was not willing to be part of that group until I received a written statement that clearly explained how the fraud had occurred. I did not receive this information.

I then initiated what became repeated requests for the original emails and data that Ariely claimed to have received from the insurance company. Within a few days, Ariely claimed that they'd been lost. Soon after, he left an audio message for me, Gino, Mazar, and Shu that included the following: "Hello to everybody . . . the first point, I should say, is that this is, if anything is wrong, it is perfectly my—my fault, and, nobody else. I was the one that was, got the connection to the, the [Ariely named the company] insurance company that ran this study . . . we gave them the instructions of what to do, and we got the data . . . Nina and I found the original data . . ." Mazar subsequently clarified that this reference to finding the original data referred to her finding the data that Ariely provided to her in February 2011.

I still do not know why, over the course of ten years, Ariely avoided my questions, fought so hard against retracting the paper, and repeatedly tried to bolster the strength of the 2012 paper, or why he asserted that the mileage data was correct when I first raised questions. While Ariely consistently clarified that he was the only author who had been in contact with the insurance company, he told BuzzFeed News that he was innocent of fraud and implied that the insurance company was responsible.[7] "I can see why it is tempting to think that I had something to do with creating the data in a fraudulent way" he said.[8] But according to BuzzFeed, Ariely gave conflicting answers about the origins of the data file that was the basis for the analysis.[9]

On July 22, 2021, Gino, Shu, and I asked *PNAS* to retract our 2012 paper. (Mazar and Ariely also made independent requests for retraction around the same time.) The media focused its attention on Ariely and released the rest of the authors from blame for committing data fraud. I am confident that people that I care about in my professional network do not view me

with suspicion, yet I remain uncomfortable about having my name connected to a fraudulent paper.

While I did not collect the insurance company data and was not directly involved in its analysis, I suspected it was problematic and shared my suspicions with my coauthors. I took their answers at face value and believed them when I should have continued to demand better answers. And when further data arrived that questioned the results of the 2012 paper, I could and should have been more persistent in highlighting my views. Being an author of a fraudulent paper haunts me, in large part due to my own complicity.

Much of this chapter has focused on the alleged field experiment at an insurance company. It is important to note, however, that the six studies showing failures to replicate, documented in the 2020 paper, more closely resembled the two laboratory studies in the 2012 paper. While I clearly believed the "signing first" effect for many years after the 2012 paper was published, the six studies in the 2020 paper changed my mind. So, how did we publish a paper in 2012 that presented this irreproducible result—in not just one laboratory experiment, but two laboratory experiments?

In retrospect, Gino reported that her lab manager at her prior university managed data collection for the two laboratory experiments in the 2012 paper. Thus, none of the authors, including me, provided sufficient supervision of these experiments. In addition, as I review emails from 2011 containing the dialogue between coauthors of the 2012 paper, I see concerns raised about the methods. I failed to actively engage and deferred to the decisions of my colleagues, and that failure makes me complicit.

While this is the only paper I have retracted due to fraud, I feel guilty about not being more closely involved in the

methods and data across my publications. I have always trusted my coauthors. Now I see the need for stronger norms of oversight to improve the integrity of the scientific process. My failure to provide that oversight created a complicity that extended beyond the "signing first" paper.

The story I've just told is not nearly as important as the stories I've told about other complicitors in this book. But it highlights the ubiquity of situations in which we are faced with a choice between being complicit and taking a stand, especially when faced with the question of whether to trust those around us. The irony of this being a story about data fraud in a paper on inducing honesty is not lost on me.

The Value and Challenge of Trust

Choosing to trust the people who surround you creates enormous opportunities in life. By trusting your colleagues, you can accomplish so much more for your organization than if you spent time rechecking all of their work or held back from sharing important information with them. Developing trust also helps us build relationships that can be key to our happiness. Thus, any concerns we may have about becoming complicit as a result of our trust in others need to be balanced against the benefits of trusting them.

One challenge associated with this balancing act is that the cues that something is wrong are typically ambiguous. When you see hints that something is wrong, it is possible that you are seeing smoke when there is no fire. Further investigation might show that no harm was done, and you could end up offending people you care about by showing your lack of trust. In academia, given all of the challenges to ensuring the integrity of data in the social sciences, I think it would be healthy if we

changed our norms to make it standard for authors to expect greater documentation of the work of their coauthors, without anyone taking offense in the process.

In an important paper on trust, organizational scholars Roger Meyer, Jim Davis, and David Schoorman highlight the power of distinguishing trust based on three different attributes of a person: their ability, their benevolence, and their integrity.[10] The scholars highlight that when you say "I trust you" to someone, that can mean that you trust the person to have the competence to complete a task (ability), the generosity required to meet their commitment (benevolence), or the intention of completing a project in an honest manner (integrity). It is easy to recall episodes in life where we trusted people based on each of these three different qualities.

Being trusting is generally a good thing. We view people who are not trusting with suspicion. It is awkward to reveal that you do not trust someone; it sounds like an accusation and can threaten the relationship. But trust can also lead to System 1 thinking, or the habit of intuitively relying on information provided by others even when we receive signals that there might be reason for concern. And, as I highlighted in chapter 3, we may be biased toward over-trusting people who are part of groups we belong to, such as our work team or our coauthors.

I trusted both the ability and the integrity of my coauthors on the 2012 paper. Reflecting on my history of interactions with my many past coauthors, I find that the only times in my career when I didn't trust a coauthor's ability were when I was mentoring a relatively new doctoral student on one of their first projects. In those cases, I would carefully review their work since they might not yet have had the skills to conduct the technical pieces of a project correctly. However, I have never paused to question the integrity of data provided by a coauthor.

And, overall, I think that being trusting has helped me complete interesting research projects and develop important professional relationships.

So, how should we integrate the benefits of trust with avoiding complicity in wrongdoing? I now think that academia should institutionalize the idea of trusting, with verification. I think that putting one's name on a paper should come with the obligation to be relatively confident that you have reason to trust the data. Checking the randomization question in the insurance-company data would have been relatively easy; I just didn't do it. Which checks are warranted will vary for different empirical papers. But the idea of trusting, with verification, would help us confront the growing number of stories about academic fraud.

By the time the 2020 replication failure paper was published, I no longer believed in the integrity of the insurance data. I was skeptical about whether a valid study had been conducted, but I did not imagine that the data were purely fraudulent. What should I have done? I could have explored the data more fully myself. I could have contacted the journal that published the 2012 paper, without the majority of my coauthors, and asked that it be retracted. In retrospect, I wish I had done this. But I didn't. Instead, by not setting the research record straight as quickly as possible, I was complicit.

After the data fraud story broke in 2021, it became clear to me that I had placed too much trust in others and, indirectly, too much trust in data presented in a paper that had my name on it. In recent years, many questions have arisen surrounding the validity and integrity of social science research, which have led to more stringent practices when it comes to conducting experiments and reporting data. We can apply these new norms to the broader question of whether it is appropriate to check the

work of our colleagues, particularly when we notice something that doesn't look right. I do not wish to become a less trusting person, but I do wish that I had listened to the signals that emerged over time in the data fraud story and questioned my trust. Being trusting may be a good attribute generally, but when we trust those who may not be worthy of our trust, we can become complicit in any harm that results.

Creating and Accepting Unethical Organizational Systems

Most of us assume that when our doctor prescribes a specific medicine for us, she believes it is the best treatment available. I personally tend to take the medicines that my internist recommends. Unfortunately, our trust may be overly optimistic, even for those of us with well-intentioned doctors. The conflicts of interest that we have accepted as a society are reason for concern, as are the complicit roles that most of us—physicians, health-care administrators, Congress, citizens, and patients— play in these conflicts of interest. We barely notice the problem, but it is a really big deal. Each year, about half of all U.S. physicians accept gifts totaling over $2 billion from the pharmaceutical industry (aka "pharma"), including meals, travel, and cash.[1]

Analyzing thirty-six studies, a team of Memorial Sloan Kettering Cancer Center medical researchers led by Dr. Aaron

Mitchell concluded that the evidence consistently shows that pharmaceutical companies' payments to doctors lead to greater prescribing of the companies' drugs.[2] The effect goes beyond drugs for minor conditions, where multiple good options exist, to critical prescription decisions involving patients with Alzheimer's, multiple sclerosis, and cancer. These gifts can lead physicians to prescribe more expensive and less efficacious drugs that have more side effects. They also increase drug costs by prompting physicians to prescribe brand-name drugs when cheaper generics are just as effective. It's not only the patients and insurers who pay these higher costs; Medicaid and Medicare go up as well, imposing a burden on taxpayers[3]

Beyond providing gifts, pharma influences physicians' decision-making through their other interactions. Pharma reps "educate" physicians about the worthiness of their company's drugs by providing them with one-sided information, a practice known as detailing. Physicians claim that they rely on pharmaceutical firms to educate them about new drugs. But research calls into question the validity and independence of the information that pharmaceutical representatives deliver to physicians through detailing.[4] As critics note, there are many superior, less biased sources of information available to doctors than that offered by self-interested pharmaceutical firms. For example, Dr. Jerry Avorn of the Harvard Medical School created Alosa Health, a nonprofit that provides physicians with free, unbiased, research-based advice about the efficacy of various drugs.[5] To maintain independence, Alosa receives no payment for its detailing-related work. Empirical studies show that such independent detailing leads to less costly and more effective prescriptions.[6]

While abundant research has established that the gifts physicians receive create a conflict of interest,[7] individual physicians

and the American Medical Association have avoided and fought opportunities to fix the problem. This resistance may be partly due to intentional self-dealing, but it also can be attributed to the widespread belief among physicians that reform is not needed because the problem is overstated.[8]

Defenders of the current system argue that relationships between physicians and industry drive innovation. It's true that research collaboration between physicians and pharma undoubtedly have the potential to create societal value by giving pharma a sense of what patients and physicians need, and what's working or not working. But the $2 billion that pharma spends on detailing has little to do with research and innovation. Rather, it's used to influence the prescriptions that physicians write.

Most (though not all) physicians are unaware of the biases that affect their prescribing behavior. They may understand that they face financial incentives to prescribe drugs and treatments that are not in their patients' best interests yet hold the false belief that since they are ethical people who would never knowingly harm a patient, they personally will not be affected by their conflict of interest. This view is consistent with how we humans tend to think about conflict of interest: as if it operates at a conscious or intentional level. Yet research both inside and outside of medicine, including my own, shows that corruption resulting from conflicts of interest is usually unintentional. When we have a vested interest in seeing a problem in a certain manner, we are no longer capable of objectivity. Parents cannot be expected to be objective about the beauty or intelligence of their children. My spouse has often accused me of having a bias toward the products and services sold by companies I consult for; she is probably correct. Similarly, doctors who receive gifts and other perks from pharma cannot be expected

to make unbiased prescribing decisions or even to be aware of the ethical dimensions of their decisions. Most will believe they are putting their patients' interests first, even as conflicts of interest bias their decisions.

Given all we know about the harmful effects of pharma payments to physicians, allowing pharma to provide gifts to physicians and physicians to accept them should be forbidden, Dr. Mitchell and his colleagues argue. Taking gifts from pharma undermines physicians' ability to live up to their oath to serve their patients' best interests, the researchers note.

Gifts and detailing are not the only ethical challenges surrounding pharma. Multiple pharmaceutical firms have been found to engage in off-label marketing, or promoting a medication for a purpose other than what the Food and Drug Administration (FDA) has approved. While doctors can legally prescribe pills for off-label use, drug companies are not allowed to market medicines for such purposes. Nonetheless, such illegal marketing occurs, and it has harmed thousands of people and defrauded Medicare and Medicaid of billions of dollars. Over thirty pharmaceutical firms have reached two or more settlements with the U.S. government over off-label marketing.

Beyond prescription writing, physicians also face other conflicts of interest. Consider the problem of whether a patient should be operated on or receive some less invasive intervention to treat their condition. Urologists who are skilled at surgery are more likely than other qualified physicians to recommend surgery for prostate cancer. Meanwhile, radiation oncologists, who use radiation therapy rather than surgery to treat prostate cancer, are more likely to recommend radiation therapy. This is true even when both groups of physicians— urologists who perform surgery and radiation oncologists—are

looking at the same patient information.[9] Both recommend the treatment modalities they provide, perceiving them to be more effective and to offer patients a better quality of life. As a result, the treatment that a patient receives for their condition depends on the type of doctor they first encounter. Each doctor is likely to be focused on advising the best possible treatment to the patient while also being biased toward a treatment plan rooted in their own area of expertise.[10] It's not that doctors are lying to patients to drum up business; clearly, they have strong convictions about their recommendations. They believe their preferred treatment is superior, and they fail to recognize that their beliefs are biased in a self-serving manner. In other words, they don't recognize that they're facing an ethical dilemma: whether to recommend *their* treatment or the *best* treatment for this patient. They fail to realize that their training, incentives, and preferences prevent them from offering objective advice.

When institutions finally confront conflicts of interest, they often assume that disclosing the problem will eliminate it. That is, they assume that if a doctor discloses her conflict of interest, the patient will be protected. Unfortunately, that's not the case. A great deal of research provides convincing evidence that disclosure is a misdirection that is likely to make matters worse rather than better. That is, when health-care professionals disclose a conflict of interest, they actually feel freer to choose actions consistent with their own self-interest, simply because they disclosed it. Moreover, the recipient of the biased advice will trust the adviser more than they would have otherwise, since the adviser was nice enough to disclose the conflict of interest.[11] This research provides an important insight for creating effective policy. Policymakers often falsely assume that disclosure will solve a problem much more than it actually will. And when they falsely assume that disclosure is sufficient to

resolve a conflict of interest, they no longer see the true need for the systemic change that is likely to be much more effective.

U.S. senator Charles Grassley (R-Iowa) has condemned medical organizations, including medical schools, for not doing more to address the conflicts of interest inherent in pharma's detailing initiatives.[12] He questions why our society continues to accept conflicts of interest that can affect life-and-death decisions. As we look for solutions, it is important to realize that much of the bias comes from well-intentioned people who believe they are making appropriate recommendations to others. Their bias is out of focus to them. Pharmaceutical firms create the environments in which physician bias can be counted on to increase sales. Policymakers who fail to fix the system are also complicit.

Obviously, the medical industry is not alone in institutionalizing unethical practices. This chapter will explore some of the ways in which we accept organizational systems without sufficient deliberation and how we may be complicit when we fail to consider organizations' role in creating harmful outcomes.

"We Only Offer Recommendations"

Some organizations are set up in a way that enables them or their leaders to take credit for successes that result from decisions made by others, while also being able to avoid blame when problems develop. Leaders often benefit from the work of subordinates and point fingers when things go wrong, as we saw in the VW story in chapter 3. Similarly, consultants are often able to deny responsibility for their clients' unethical behavior and take credit when they behave well. As a consultant, I myself am privileged to be in a position to offer advice to organizations on negotiation, decision-making, and ethics

without having to bear the burden of making the final decisions that are required and facing their consequences. Many of us who benefit financially under this arrangement fail to consider our complicity if our advice contributes to wrongdoing by those we advise. Since our involvement in the wrongdoing is indirect, we are at risk of ducking blame and responsibility.

In chapter 1, I highlighted consulting firm McKinsey's role in the opioid crisis. As it turns out, McKinsey has offered advice in many other domains that create net harm to the world. One of these is the insurance industry. When you pay a premium to an insurance company, what do you expect when a bad event that you were insured against happens, such as a house fire or a car crash, and you make an honest claim? For most of the history of the insurance industry, you could have assumed that if such a bad event happened, you would file a claim, and the insurance company would simply pay its fair value. Today, though, when you file a claim after a car accident, the insurance company might offer you an amount far below the fair market value of the claim. In frustration, you might hire an attorney to dispute the decision. As the dispute gets more complicated and contentious, both sides accrue mounting costs in fighting the claim. After a couple of years, a week before the trial is set to start, you might follow your attorney's advice to settle with the insurance company. Then you can expect your attorney to take one-third of whatever you accept from the insurance company.

How did the claims process get so complicated and unpleasant? Your insurance company would likely tell you that it needs to defend itself against fraudulent claims. But a more significant explanation is probably linked to advice provided by McKinsey. In his book *Delay, Deny, Defend*, Jay Feinman traces the complications, deception, and dishonesty inherent in today's insurance industry to 1992, when Allstate hired McKinsey to

provide "advice" on its claims process.[13] Focused exclusively on maximizing its client's profits, McKinsey argued for changing the existing industry norm of trying to pay the fair value of the claim to treating each claim as a zero-sum game, where each extra dollar paid was good for the claimant but bad for Allstate. Essentially, McKinsey consultants advised Allstate to change the claims process from meeting its moral obligation to their customers to a profit center, where the goal became finding ways to persuade claimants to accept the lowest settlement possible.

The specific tactics that McKinsey recommended included lowballing customers with "take it or leave it" offers and delaying payment to make many claimants more desperate for cash, which increased their willingness to take what they could get quickly. From Allstate's perspective, McKinsey's advice worked: after lowering the amount paid on claims, the company saw its profits soar. Based on its success at helping Allstate reduce its integrity and increase profits, McKinsey sold similar advice to State Farm, Farmers, Liberty Mutual, and other leading insurance firms.[14] McKinsey had created and distributed a formula to increase dishonest profits and destroy the integrity of the industry. By the way, as McKinsey would be the first to tell you: it was the executives at the insurance firms who chose to change their claims processes. McKinsey only offered advice.

McKinsey's consulting work for the government of Saudi Arabia also highlights its complicity in wrongdoing. According to an extensive report in the *New Yorker*, the Saudi government hired McKinsey in 2018 to measure public perceptions of "certain Saudi economic policies."[15] McKinsey's report identified a journalist and a dissident who were supposedly responsible for negative coverage of the government's policies on Twitter.[16] Soon after, the Saudi government arrested the journalist and a

brother of the dissident and shut down the anonymous Twitter feed. The same year, Saudi journalist Jamal Khashoggi was brazenly killed by Saudi agents at the Saudi consulate in Istanbul in retaliation for his criticism of the regime. To take another example, in 2020, McKinsey was accused of helping Isabel dos Santos, the daughter of Angola's former president, launder state funds.[17] Santos became a billionaire by transferring government funds through shell companies and on to tax havens. McKinsey provided the know-how that enabled the scheme.

McKinsey operated in Russia for nearly thirty years before Russia launched its 2022 war on Ukraine. Employing more than seven hundred people, McKinsey had engagements with twenty-one of the country's biggest firms, including Kremlin-controlled companies under Western government sanctions like Rosneft, Gazprom, and VEB Bank. In the days after Russia attacked Ukraine on February 24, McKinsey resisted joining the hordes of Western businesses and governments unequivocally cutting economic ties with Russia. In a February 27 LinkedIn post, McKinsey global managing partner Bob Sternfels wrote only that the firm, which had previously ended engagements with the Kremlin, would no longer work for any local or regional governments in Russia. Current and former McKinsey staff members, including the head of McKinsey's Ukrainian office, harshly criticized the firm's decision to continue serving its many other Russian clients. "You should be ashamed," former McKinsey senior partner Andrei Caramitro wrote in a LinkedIn post. "It's blood money on your hands."[18] In response to the controversy, McKinsey announced it would "immediately cease existing work with state-owned entities" and take on no new client work in Russia, but that it would conclude its "remaining engagements." (By comparison, consulting firm Accenture, which had 2,300 employees in Russia, said it would

discontinue all of its business there.) In an email the previous year, the managing partner of McKinsey's Moscow office, Vitaly Klintsov, banned employees from attending a protest for jailed opposition leader Alexei Navalny, Russian president Vladimir Putin's fiercest critic, and from posting their political views on social media. The email attracted widespread condemnation, with Republican senator Marco Rubio saying that it "raises serious questions about McKinsey's core values and corporate culture." As Sternfels did a year later, Klintsov responded by reversing course: McKinsey fully supported employees' right to engage in "civil and political activities," he said.[19]

McKinsey defends itself by noting that it has also helped companies and countries develop policies that have created jobs, improved education, and alleviated poverty. I believe this. But this does not morally justify the firm's choice to offer advice that its leaders know will intentionally harm customers and citizens, destroy the integrity of entire industries, and support dictatorships. McKinsey's claim that it only offers advice may provide legal protection, but it does not create moral dispensation. McKinsey has been repeatedly complicit in wrongdoing and has an ethical obligation to develop more rigorous protocols for assessing the morality of its engagements. Of course, it is important to note that McKinsey is far from the only consulting firm that provides assistance to those who create harm.

When organizations contribute to and benefit from the wrongdoing of others, they are complicit in the harm created. I try to take this idea seriously by refusing to provide consulting services that I believe would impose net harm on society—even if I only offered advice and didn't make final decisions. I hope that more advisers and organizations will begin to consider the potential impact of their advice not only on their clients and themselves, but on all of us.

When Goals Drive Out Ethics

Goal setting is one of the most popular management tools around. This isn't surprising, given that hundreds of studies show that challenging goals can powerfully improve performance.[20] Enthusiasts of goal setting argue for setting specific and challenging goals, such as "Sell 10 million cars per year," "Reduce costs by 25%," or "Sell eight products to every customer." Numerous studies show that specific, challenging goals lead to higher performance than vaguer "Do your best" goals.[21]

But goal setting can prompt employees to develop a narrow view of what they are trying to accomplish, such that unmeasured attributes of performance move out of focus and are ignored. For instance, if you set a goal focused on quantity of performance, quality may well suffer.[22] In my industry, if a university made tenure decisions primarily based on the number of papers professors published, this goal would motivate professors to publish more papers, but our teaching and service activities might decline. Other research finds that firms issuing quarterly earnings reports frequently meet or beat analyst expectations but often do so by cutting expenses in research and development. Short-term targets are achieved at the expense of long-term growth.[23]

One striking example of how instructing people to focus on one dimension of a goal can lead them to overlook other information can be seen in Dan Simons and Chris Chabris's well-known video on inattentional blindness.[24] In the video, two groups of players, one wearing white T-shirts and the other wearing dark T-shirts, are passing basketballs. Viewers of the video are given the specific, challenging goal of counting basketball passes among people wearing only white T-shirts. Not surprisingly, people assigned this task ignore the black-shirted

individuals. And as a result of focusing on the white-shirted players, viewers also usually fail to notice something else: a person in a black gorilla suit walking across the middle of the screen, pounding their chest, and then walking off screen. The goal of counting passes leads people to overlook the obvious.

In a similar manner, focusing on moderately difficult goals can lead employees to act unethically. In their research, Maurice Schweitzer, Lisa Ordóñez, and Bambi Douma found that study participants who were asked to self-report their performance were more likely to exaggerate how well they'd done when they faced a specific, challenging goal than when they did not, especially when their actual performance level fell just short of reaching the goal.[23] The focus on goal achievement led the ethical dimension of the task to fade from view, a process that Notre Dame professor Ann Tenbrunsel has termed "ethical fading."[26]

Turning from the laboratory to the real world, many of the most visible recent corporate scandals were rooted in specific, challenging goals. We have already covered Volkswagen's Dieselgate scandal in some detail, but it's important to note that chairman Ferdinand Piëch and CEO Martin Winterkorn set a sales target of ten million cars a year and that employees felt enormous pressure to achieve this goal. The goal was a core motivator of employees' decisions to cheat and lie to the world about their vehicles' emissions, decisions that led to many deaths and widespread suffering. Years before Dieselgate unfolded, Schweitzer and his colleagues predicted and found that specific, challenging goals would increase the likelihood of unethical behavior in pursuit of such goals.

In recent years, a similar relationship between goal setting and misconduct developed at Wells Fargo Bank. Between 2009 and 2016, Wells Fargo fraudulently opened 3.5 million

accounts for its customers without their authorization and also enrolled 528,000 customers for online bill-payment services, again without their authorization.[27] In 2016, when the media uncovered the fraud, senior management claimed that it comprised unrelated offenses by individual branch employees. To underscore their own innocence, upper management fired 5,300 lower-level employees for the fraudulent activity.

In fact, senior management fostered the illegal behavior by setting sales goals that were very difficult, if not impossible, to achieve honestly. A 2017 report by the Independent Directors of the Board of Wells Fargo concluded that the fraud had been a broad organizational failure rather than a set of individual failures. Richard Kovacevich, the CEO of Wells Fargo, developed the motto "Go for Gr-Eight," which pushed employees to sell eight products per customer—four times the average rate for banks.[28] Kovacevich left the CEO position in 2007 but stayed on as chairman for two more years, and his unrealistic goal setting continued. Each Wells Fargo branch, or "store," as Kovacevich preferred to call them, would set ambitious sales goals that encouraged employees to sell clients products they did not need and never requested but for which they were charged new fees.[29]

Front-line employees who failed to meet their goals were coached to increase their sales beyond a level that could be achieved honestly.[30] Fearing they would lose their jobs, many Wells Fargo employees began engaging in illegal and unethical behaviors to meet goals, including signing clients up for new accounts without their knowledge.[31] In one sad case, a homeless person was convinced to open six bank accounts that cost $39 per month in fees.[32]

Though Wells Fargo had established a system in which employees would face harsh reprisals for failing to meet

unattainable goals, senior employees blamed individual employees who were caught breaking the law. Employees were also fired for trying to report the illegal practices to the company's ethics hotline.[33] The collective pattern shows that the illegalities at Wells Fargo were driven by the unrealistic goals set by upper management.

I am personally bothered by an apparent relationship between goal setting and unethical action at multinational London-based oil and gas company British Petroleum (BP). From 2005 to 2006, I spent forty-two days consulting with BP, training the company's top seventy-five executives on diplomacy and negotiation. I focused on teaching the executives how to negotiate in places around the globe that follow very different rules and laws than those found in the United States and the United Kingdom.

While I was working with BP's senior executives, the company faced disasters in the United States. You likely remember the explosion of the BP-chartered *Deepwater Horizon* drilling rig in April 2010, which caused a massive oil leak in the Gulf of Mexico, the worst human-created environmental disaster in history. This spill took place while Tony Hayward was the company's CEO, years after I ended my consulting work with BP. But in March 2005, while I was working with BP, an explosion at a BP refinery in Texas City, Texas, killed 15 and injured 170 more. Just a year later, in March 2006, a BP pipeline in the Prudhoe Bay Oil Field on Alaska's North Slope leaked 267,000 gallons of crude oil on the frozen tundra. Lord John Browne was the CEO during the Texan and Alaskan disasters and during the time I consulted with BP.

Clearly, massive leadership failures contributed to all three of these crises. Many accounts have suggested that BP's culture failed to value worker safety and protection of the natural

environment.[34] However, I did not observe such deficiencies on my many visits to London. In fact, on my first visit to London in 2005, soon before the Texas City fire, I was immediately struck by BP's obsession with safety, down to the smallest detail. For example, before I could enter corporate headquarters or any hotel where training took place, I was given a thorough briefing about evacuation plans in the event of a problem in the building. I also recall that when a very senior BP executive visited Harvard to give a series of talks, he refused to cross on a red light as we walked across campus because doing so would violate BP's safety practices. We were running late for the executive's public presentation, but in his view, that was no excuse for jaywalking, even though there weren't any cars around.

Many people viewed John Browne, BP's CEO at the time, as a bold visionary who cared about the environment. In a landmark speech at Stanford University in 1997, Browne broke ranks within the oil industry by becoming the first CEO of a global oil company to acknowledge the risk posed by climate change. Under Browne's leadership, BP pledged to take bold action to respond to the threat. Certainly, some questioned the sincerity of Browne's commitment. But based on my own observations of BP's actions, including the company's significant investments in alternative fuels, I am confident that Browne's 1997 speech about the environment was sincere and that he was honestly committed to changing BP's focus on oil. Moreover, in 2005–2006, I was thoroughly convinced that the majority of BP's senior executives were proud of the firm's commitment to the environment at that time. I realize that this sounds bizarre, given all we now know about the disaster in the Gulf and the company's other crises.

How does my belief in BP leaders' commitment to safety and the environment square with the trio of disasters? I believe

other goals got in the way. Browne and the senior executive team were committed to the environment and to safety, but they also wanted to cut costs. In 1999, Browne set the goal of reducing spending by 25 percent across the board. That same year, BP pleaded guilty to a felony conviction of illegal dumping at the Prudhoe Bay Oil Field in 1995. To avoid having its government contracts in Alaska canceled, BP entered a five-year probationary period with the Environmental Protection Agency, during which it had to undertake significant reforms to reduce environmental risks and improve regulatory compliance. Less than a year later, employees complained to an independent arbitrator that BP was failing to maintain equipment and safety systems at the Alaska oil field. "There is a disconnect between . . . management's stated commitment to safety and the perception of that commitment," a panel of independent experts hired by BP to investigate the allegations concluded in a 2001 operational integrity report.[35] Nonetheless, in 2004, Browne set another goal for a round of massive budget cuts. "The focus on controlling costs was acute at BP, to the point it became a distraction," one BP manager said. "They just go after it with a ferocity that's mind-numbing and terrifying. No one's ever asked to cut corners or take a risk, but often it ends up like that."[36]

What happened at BP? The evidence suggests that cost-cutting goals played a crucial role in its safety issues.[37] Those at the highest levels of the corporation were focused on safety and the environment but also set clear, measurable goals on cost cutting. As their messages crossed the ocean to Alaska and the Gulf, the quantitative metric appears to have squeezed out more amorphous safety and environmental goals. For lower-level employees instructed to focus on cost-cutting, it seems likely that concerns about safety and the environment faded from their focus.

Was I complicit in the disasters at BP? Certainly not intentionally, and much of the specific advice I offered was aimed at promoting ethical behavior. I thought at the time that the organization was ethical, but did I miss important signals? I'm not sure I will ever know the true answer. But I do think that I could have been more careful about considering whether my views were influenced by my desire to see my client in a positive light.

At VW, Wells Fargo, and BP, senior leadership's obsession with employees reaching specific, challenging goals contributed to ethical concerns drifting out of employees' focus and inspired massive unethical and illegal actions. The senior executives who set the unreasonable goals and the mid-level managers who transmitted them down the hierarchy were extremely complicit in the behavior of employees who directly lied and cheated, even though the executives and managers often had never met these employees.

Creating, Claiming, and Accepting False Independence

Boards of directors of public companies are expected to represent the interest of the companies' shareholders. In the United States, to help make that happen, boards are expected to ensure that a majority of board members are "independent." A director is typically defined as independent if they (1) do not have a material relationship with the company that could keep them from exercising their independent judgment, (2) are not part of the company's executive team, and (3) are not involved with the company's day-to-day operations. The expectation is that the independent majority of directors will be likely to consider the best interests of shareholders first and not be swayed by

the individual goals of the CEO and management team, such as maximizing their income.

I fully appreciate the goal of ensuring that boards of public companies have independent directors. In too many recent scandals—Theranos and The Weinstein Company being extreme examples—boards should have noticed the wrongdoing and acted long before the scandals became public, but they were packed with insiders who had incentives not to notice. Companies should attempt to eliminate the conflicts of interest of independent directors who represent shareholders but are motivated to please senior management. Yet the phrase "independent board members" is a deceptive misnomer. The truth is that most board members—including those deemed "independent"—are selected with the encouragement and/or approval of the CEO and/or senior management team, and these board members are often rewarded for supporting the senior executive team.

Many professionals face a conflict of interest between what is best for them financially and what is in the best interest of a group of people they represent. Just as physicians have financial incentives to recommend the treatments they specialize in, attorneys may have incentives to either go to court or to avoid court, incentives that may not match their clients' interests. As I've described, when we are motivated to see information in a particular manner, we are no longer capable of being independent or objective. In fact, as I highlighted earlier, people who disclose their conflicts of interest act in an even more biased and self-serving manner than those who do not.[38] Similarly, when we read that outside directors are "independent," we likely become more willing to defer to these experts, assuming they will try to protect us, even when they continue to share the bias of the top leadership team.[39]

Beyond corporate boards of directors, the adjective "independent" is even more central to the world of corporate audits. Most Western economies require that the financial statements of corporations be audited by an "independent auditor." This requirement is intended to give other parties faith in the honesty of the company's financial statements. In a majority opinion of the Supreme Court in 1984, Chief Justice Warren Burger articulated the importance of auditor independence:

> The independent auditor assumes a public responsibility transcending any employment relationship with the client. The independent public accountant performing this special function owes ultimate allegiance to the company's creditors and stockholders, as well as to [the] investing public. This "public watchdog" function demands that the accountant maintain total independence from the client at all times and requires complete fidelity to the public trust.[40]

The auditing profession claims to support this view. "In the performance of any professional service, a member must maintain objectivity and integrity, shall be free of conflicts of interest, and shall not knowingly misrepresent facts," states the American Institute of Certified Public Accountants Code of Professional Conduct.[41] But in 1997, Kimberly Morgan, George Loewenstein, and I argued that massive conflicts of interest existed in the structure of the auditing industry and that auditors failed the independence test suggested by Chief Justice Burger. A quarter century later, my view is that auditors are still not independent, are biased to please their clients, and are affected by conflicts of interest. I believe that the industry's use of the adjective "independent" constitutes a misleading and fraudulent claim.

Auditors are not independent because they have strong incentives to keep their clients happy. Auditors want to maintain

their clients, to sell additional services to them, and often even to seek jobs from them in the future. While most auditors do not intentionally corrupt audits, it is not possible for them to be completely unbiased. Creating true auditor independence would require fundamental changes to the structure of the relationship between auditors and their clients, such that auditors are not "partners" of their clients but rather act as true judges of companies' financial statements. As in the other industries we've considered in this chapter, individual auditors are not the central villains. Rather, leadership of the largest accounting firms, which spend millions of dollars each year lobbying Congress to keep it from enacting a truly independent system, is complicit.

Mirroring the audit industry, consider the role of credit-rating agencies in the lead-up to the 2008 financial crisis. The core task of credit-rating agencies is to educate outside stakeholders of the creditworthiness of issuers of debt obligations, such as banks and insurance companies, and the debt instruments these financial organizations sell to the public. During the housing bubble that preceded the Great Recession, many debt issuers began to bundle and sell subprime loans as mortgage-backed securities. After the crisis, the House Oversight and Government Reform Committee found evidence that executives at the rating agencies were "well aware that there was little basis for giving AAA ratings to thousands of increasingly complex mortgage-related securities, but the companies often vouched for them anyway," according to the committee's chairman, Representative Henry Waxman.[42]

Credit-rating agency executives testified before the House committee that a conflict of interest made it difficult for the U.S. credit-rating system to perform as intended. Like the audit firms, the largest credit-rating agencies—Standard & Poor's,

Moody's, and Fitch—are paid by the companies they rate rather than by the investors who have a true stake in the ratings. The more rigorous its standards, the less attractive a credit-rating agency becomes to its clients. And, like the major U.S. auditing firms, the allegedly independent credit-rating agencies worked hard to sell consulting services to the very same clients. Independence is core to why credit-rating agencies exist, yet their compensation structure displays an inherent conflict of interest.

Fixing Corrupted Environments

The well-intentioned prescribing physician, the surgeon who believes that operating is the best treatment, the bank employee who wants to boost sales, and the auditor or consultant who seeks to please the client are complicit, not the core complicitors. The actors who created, institutionalized, and accepted these corrupt systems are far more complicit. When we witness a relatively low-level employee acting in a manner that departs from ethical behavior, we need to look beyond that person's behavior and think about the more senior people who were involved in creating the institutions that led to these predictably unethical behaviors.

Acting on Complicity

9

The Psychology of Complicity

Why do people enable the harmful behaviors of others? The answer to this question largely depends on the profile of complicity to which people belong. True partners and collaborators have very different bases for complicity than the other groups we have discussed. True partners of the Nazi Party shared Hitler's hatred of communists, socialists, homosexuals, and Jews, and supported all or many of the views he expressed in *Mein Kampf*. We discussed these evil true partners in chapter 2. Many other collaborators are willing to support a harm doer in exchange for benefits that they expect to obtain on other issues. Thus, while Trump's discriminatory policies against Muslims, African Americans, Mexicans, and the Chinese were consistent with the preferences of some of his true partners, like Steve Bannon, other members of his coalition supported Trump for other reasons, such as the desire to restrict access to abortion, get massive tax breaks, and benefit from more lax government regulation. The actions of true partners and collaborators are typically intentional, and little complex psychological theory is required to explain their behavior.

I expect that most readers of this book do not see themselves as the partners or collaborators of evildoers. But my guess is that as we discussed the other profiles of complicity, you may have recognized some of your past behaviors, as I have. Why do we engage in less intentional but significant forms of complicity? This chapter explores the psychology behind such complicity.

Single Sourcing of Blame

What caused the massive fraud at Theranos? Please write down your answer, and take as much time as you need.

I recently gave this task to a group of very senior executives from all around the world, across lots of industries, in an executive program that I was teaching at Harvard Business School. A couple of months before, they had participated in a full class discussion of the Theranos case with one of my colleagues. They talked about the role of Theranos's board in allowing the fraud to develop, the role of the venture capital investors, and the role that Walgreens played in bringing the company's fraudulent testing equipment into its stores. The class also discussed the role that Sunny Balwani, the president of Theranos and Elizabeth Holmes's romantic partner, played in creating and maintaining the fraudulent organization.

Because of the COVID-19 pandemic, I was teaching this group of executives online. I asked the class what caused the massive fraud at Theranos; each executive was asked to enter their answer in the chat function. The time allowed was generous. Clearly, there were multiple causes of the fraud at Theranos. But when I looked at the class's answers, I found they tended to be simple and singular. Sixty-two of the seventy responses offered a single cause, and fifty-six of those sixty-two were a simple description of Elizabeth Holmes, such as her ego or lack of integrity. The

other six single-cause explanations had to do with the board's failure to provide effective governance. Only eight of seventy responses mentioned two causes—either two simple descriptors of Holmes or one descriptor of Holmes plus the board's failure. No mention was made of the role of the venture capital firms in boosting and supporting Theranos, Walgreens's lack of due diligence before putting Theranos technology in its stores, or the board's lack of expertise in medicine and technology. In other words, the vast majority of the sophisticated executives in my class, who knew all aspects of the story, blamed a single source.

When attributing blame for scandals, most of us tend to center in on a single explanation. This propensity to look for one cause extends beyond scandals. University of Chicago marketing professor Ann McGill has highlighted the fallacy of a single-cause mindset with the example of people arguing endlessly about the cause of teenage pregnancies.[1] Those on the right tend to see the cause as teenage promiscuity, while those on the left focus on lack of birth control. Yet, if you ask a biologist which explanation is correct, the biologist will say both are! As this example shows, single sourcing of blame is often politically motivated.

In a 2019 *Psychology Today* article, psychologist Steven Rathje implicates the media, which tends to deliver simple, bite-sized explanations, for our narrow focus on a single cause of news events.[2] As an example, he cites the Vox article "A New Study Reveals the Real Reason Obama Voters Switched to Trump,"[3] which gives the impression that there is only one answer to this complex phenomenon. In a set of carefully controlled studies, Princeton psychologist Tania Lombrozo found that people are more likely to believe simple, single-cause explanations for fictional events than equally plausible explanations with two causes.[4] We find simple ideas preferable

because they allow us to believe that we thoroughly know and understand a phenomenon, according to Swedish physician Hans Rosling.[5] This tendency is dangerous, he argues, because it allows us to falsely assume that complex problems can be solved with a single solution.

The fallacy of a single cause also crops up in the context of enduring disputes. When you ask people why a difficult conflict persists, they typically come up with a single explanation that focuses on the inappropriate behavior of the other side. So, Palestinians and far-left Americans are likely to blame the repressive policies of the Israeli occupiers for the failure to achieve Middle East peace. In contrast, right-leaning Israelis and Americans are more likely to focus on the failure of Palestinians to accept peace when they have been offered it in the past. Neither side tends to be willing to acknowledge what "their" side has done to contribute to the dispute.

I confess that if I had been asked to answer my own question about what caused the massive fraud at Theranos six months before I started writing this book, I can easily imagine that I would have provided a simple, single explanation that focused on Elizabeth Holmes. I like simplicity, or what academics sometimes call parsimony. This preference for parsimony is consistent with the famous philosophical principle known as Occam's razor, which argues that when we are faced with two scientific explanations for a phenomenon, the simplest explanation is usually the most accurate one. While it is true that simpler explanations are easier to communicate, there is no evidence to support Occam's razor as a rule of thumb that can be widely applied. In the stories I have told throughout this book, simple explanations are insufficient accounts of what happened.

The fallacy of a single cause explains not only why we tend to focus on a core wrongdoer when assigning blame but also

why we ignore the role of this person's complicitors. Single sourcing of blame for wrongdoing too easily lets those who are complicit off the hook, which can keep us from fixing complicit institutions and eliminating our own complicity in the future.

Implicating complicitors requires a complex, multifaceted account of a story. Those of us who want to tell stories more accurately and contribute to solving problems would be wise to ask questions such as, "What were some of the factors that caused the massive fraud at Theranos?" rather than, "What caused the massive fraud at Theranos?" The former question is more likely to prompt us to think about all of the causes of the event that we are trying to understand.

Single sourcing of blame is just one psychological explanation for our complicity with wrongdoing. In the rest of the chapter, we will explore the psychology of indirect harm, why our complicity is so easily out of focus, the role of the omission bias, how wrongdoing often evolves on a slippery slope, and the role of fear.

The Psychology of Indirect Harm

When people deliberately steal, lie, or cheat, they often do so to gain some direct benefit, such as money, a job, or a favor. We can also benefit through our inaction, as when we don't take the time to notice our privilege and receive indirect benefits that the system provides to some people and not others. As we've seen, for example, privilege can lead people to engage in behaviors that perpetuate racial inequities, such as requesting special favors, accepting racially biased laws and rules, and ignoring the preferences of people of color. Ample research evidence shows that when we create harm indirectly and benefit from that harm, we more readily justify it than when we create harm

directly.[6] To take another example, when we see a boss benefit from harm perpetuated by a subordinate, we often fail to notice the pretty obvious possibility that the subordinate committed wrongdoing for the benefit of the boss.

We fail to hold indirect harm doers accountable when they do their dirty work through others, Boston College economics professor Lucas Coffman has shown.[7] In his experiments, he used a classic economics game called the dictator game. Traditionally, the game involves a study participant in the role of "dictator" deciding how to divide up a certain amount of money between themselves and a "receiver." Despite having the opportunity to keep all of the funds, participants in the role of dictator often share some, or even half, of the money with the powerless receiver out of a desire to be fair. In his experiments, Coffman inserted an intermediary between the dictator and the recipient. Specifically, the dictator could "hire" an intermediary to make a decision on their behalf. The intermediary had the ability to act selfishly on behalf of themselves and the dictator. In Coffman's experiments, the intermediary treats the powerless recipient far worse than dictators do when allocating on their own behalf. Nonetheless, observers of all of this activity generally do not hold the dictator accountable for the selfishness that they controlled.

Unfortunately, the human mind does not hold people fully responsible for the indirect harm that they create. As a result, we let advisers off of the moral hook, which encourages them to feel comfortable contributing to harm.

When Complicity Is Out of Focus

In the previous chapter, I described Dan Simons and Chris Chabris's well-known video on inattentional blindness, which is often used to demonstrate how focusing on one dimension

of a problem can lead us to miss other important information.[8] When people are assigned the specific, challenging goal of counting basketball passes among only players wearing white T-shirts, most viewers fail to notice when a person in a black gorilla suit walks across the middle of the screen, pounds their chest, and walks off screen.

While not seeing the gorilla doesn't create any actual harm, other cases of not noticing have more serious performance and ethical implications. When an ethical scandal or crime hits the news, many people claimed they knew something fishy was going on. After Bernie Madoff was found to have run a multi-year Ponzi scheme that took in over $20 billion from his investors, for example, many in the financial industry claimed that they never trusted Madoff's reported returns. So, why didn't they say so earlier? When we are focused on other aspects of a situation or a decision, such as maximizing profits or selling more products, the ethical dimension may slip out of view, or ethically fade."[9]

Avoiding complicity can be even more challenging when we work closely with the wrongdoer or have a social relationship with them, as in the case of my consulting relationship with BP. The wrongdoer we observe is often someone we know, like, and want to succeed—our boss, colleague, customer, supplier, or even a family member or friend. Thus, the same motivational blindness that so-called independent directors, auditors, and credit raters experience when they are assigned to make objective assessments may be even more pronounced when we are close to those engaged in wrongdoing. Our relationships can blind us to their unethical actions and allow them to continue inflicting harm.

In many cases of wrongdoing, the core harm doer actively wants to keep others from noticing or acting on their ethical

violations. Like a magician, they distract us from seeing their evil acts by focusing our attention elsewhere—such as on the lofty mission of their organization or their seemingly dazzling innovations. Both Adam Neumann of WeWork and Elizabeth Holmes of Theranos followed this pattern. Such evildoers often suggest that the world is at a profound tipping point and the old rules no longer apply, an argument meant to put any potential criticisms or concerns to rest. Rather than being appeased by such claims, our ethical warning system should go on high alert.

Harm doers often obscure their behavior by playing up their competition with an "enemy." That enemy might be new immigrants, our company's archrival in its industry, an opposing sports team, or a nation we're fighting in a war. When unethical actions are focused on beating the competition, many supporters will simply not notice them. If it will help our team win, we will ignore media reports of those on "our side" stealing signals from opponents, abusing their partners, or, like football star Michael Vick, killing dogs. We need to realize that unethical behavior is not justifiable simply because the wrongdoer is on our "team" and that when we act like it is, we become a complicitor.

The Omission Bias

Imagine that you think that someone in your firm is violating company policy and the law, but you aren't certain. You have heard rumors that they are receiving kickbacks from a supplier in exchange for purchasing from the supplier. And you personally have observed your colleague engaged in patterns of behavior that don't make much sense unless they are engaged in wrongdoing. However, you don't have direct evidence of any wrongdoing, and you basically like your colleague. Further, such wrongdoing would violate company policy and the law,

but unless it becomes known, it actually helps your company. What will you do? Act on your suspicion, or "mind your own business"?

Let's back up and consider the action/no-action decision without the complicity angle. Imagine that it's a couple of years from now, and a new and dangerous strain of the coronavirus has developed. You have a 10 percent chance of catching this new strain. A vaccine is available that is 95 percent effective at preventing severe illness and death from the new strain, though the vaccine is often associated with temporary unpleasant side effects, such as fever and fatigue. The consensus within the scientific community is that you are much safer with the vaccine than without it. Would you get the vaccine? As we saw in 2021 after highly effective COVID-19 vaccines became available, many people would not. Often, that is because they were more concerned about the risk of action than about the risk of inaction, even when the risk of inaction is objectively higher.[10] Psychologists Ilana Ritov and Jon Baron describe this irrational preference for harms of omission (inaction) over harms of commission (action) as the omission bias. When weighing risky choices, where one option requires you to do something and the other option is to do nothing, people often follow the rule of thumb "Do no harm." The problem is that sometimes the wisest and most ethical action requires us to risk some harm (getting vaccinated) to avoid a far greater harm (such as getting COVID-19), or to accept some harm to create massive benefits for other people or on other dimensions. The omission bias partially explains why so many people are reluctant to receive vaccines, despite their amazing effectiveness and track record for safety over time.

Many readers will be familiar with the famous philosophy problem known as the "footbridge dilemma," in which you are

asked to imagine that you are standing on a footbridge over a trolley track next to a railway worker wearing a large backpack.[11] Below you, a runaway trolley is headed toward five innocent people standing on the track. You realize that you could save the five people by pushing the worker off the bridge and onto the tracks below. The man would die, and his body would stop the trolley from hitting the five others. In Trolleyland, you would face no legal repercussions for such an action, and all outcomes are 100 percent certain: if you push the man, he dies; if you don't push him, five people die. What would you do?[12]

People's choices in this scenario typically follow one of two different philosophies, utilitarianism or deontology. Utilitarianism focuses on doing the greatest good for the greatest number of people, such as finding a way for one person to die rather than five. Deontology, meanwhile, judges the morality of an action based on its adherence to rules or duties—such as the rule that you should not push people off of bridges into oncoming trains.[13] I won't try to resolve this fundamental philosophical debate in my book on complicity, but suffice to say that the more popular decision is to not push the guy off the bridge. This choice, which does not maximize the collective good that can be done in this situation, is consistent with the omission bias, or the tendency to weigh the harm caused by action more than the harm caused by inaction. Maximizing the greatest good for the greatest number is not universally accepted as an ethical goal, and deontologists and some legal scholars believe that there are important differences between acts of omission and acts of commission. But, at a minimum, I think we should be aware when we allow harm to be done through an act of omission.

Returning to the issue of complicity, we are often complicit through our inaction. When we do nothing in response to evil,

or facilitate evil by simply going about our business, we are complicit. This type of complicity is consistent with psychological research showing our bias toward inaction. In the realm of complicity, bias toward inaction is exacerbated by uncertainty. When we aren't certain that someone is engaged in unethical activity but think they probably are, the idea of accusing them feels risky, awkward, and potentially harmful. After all, what if we're wrong? Our uncertainty leads us to say nothing and become complicit. But rather than accepting this uncertainty and moving on, we should be motivated to learn more.

In my 2014 book *The Power of Noticing*, I document my most vivid personal experience with not speaking up.[14] In the busiest months of my life, I was serving as an expert witness for the U.S. Department of Justice (DOJ) in a fraud and racketeering case against the tobacco industry. As I was preparing to testify in court, an attorney for the DOJ asked me to change my testimony in ways that would make it less aggressive toward the tobacco industry. The request made little sense to me. I was told that the number-three official at the DOJ, Associate Attorney General Robert D. McCallum Jr.—a George W. Bush appointee who had been a partner at a firm that represented the R. J. Reynolds Tobacco Company—was threatening to remove me from the case and not allow me to testify. I found the request disturbing and refused to change my testimony, but I also failed to notify anyone about this seemingly bizarre request. I didn't call the press, demand to talk to a higher-ranked DOJ official, or call ethical attorneys I knew in D.C. to help me better understand what was happening. I was inactive.

About seven weeks after the trial ended, the *New York Times* reported that McCallum had tried to weaken the testimony of another expert witness in the case, Campaign for Tobacco-Free Kids president Matthew Myers, as part of a broader effort to

corruptly weaken the DOJ's own case. Myers was courageous in speaking out about the attempted witness tampering, while I was complicit through my inaction (though I did tell my story to the *Washington Post* after being nudged by Myers's story).

When confronted with the bizarre request, I certainly didn't know what was going on or that evil was involved. And, with these facts in mind, many people who hear my story conclude that I did nothing wrong. I disagree. I think that I had a moral obligation to try to learn more. Many journalists have told me that when a situation doesn't make sense, that's often where the most interesting stories can be found, if you're willing to dig. I could have and should have searched more to find out if I was involved with evil. My inaction made me complicit.

"The decision to do nothing is as much an act as the decision to do something," writes Amos Guiora in *Armies of Enablers,* speaking of the complicitors who facilitated the Holocaust and the crimes of sexual predators, including Catholic priests and Larry Nassar. "If we do not acknowledge this, we let the person who chose not to act off of the hook in excusing their behavior."[15] Guiora goes on to recommend the criminalization of complicity, a theme I will return to in chapter 11.

The Slippery Slope to Complicity

One explanation for the fact that a majority of Republicans in Congress supported Trump's attempt to overturn the results of the 2020 election, including the violent January 6 siege of the Capitol, is that they were simply escalating their behavior of the prior four years, such that their support was just one more step in their complicit and corrupt behavior.[16] The Republicans' backing of the coup attempt is a perfect demonstration of how toxic environments grow gradually, beginning with

minor instances of problematic behavior that then continues and expands, argues psychologist Catherine Sanderson.[17]

Sanderson cites my coauthored research showing that study participants playing the role of financial auditors are more willing to accept the corrupt behavior of their clients when it develops incrementally than when it switches abruptly from honest to corrupt. When ethical behavior deteriorates in this manner, along a slippery slope, others are less likely to notice and report unethical actions.[18] Many have asked how auditor Arthur Anderson certified Enron's corrupt financial statements year after year. One possible answer, consistent with our research, is that Enron increased its corruption gradually each year, on a slippery slope. The first year, the corruption might have been just barely permissible. The next year, it might have just crossed the line into unethical and unlawful behavior. By the time the fraud escalated to become glaringly obvious, the company's auditors might have simply gotten used to it.[19] People are more willing to engage in unethical conduct when they have the opportunity to gradually increase their level of unethicality, Arizona State University management school professor David Welsh and his colleagues have found.[20] This research helps explain Republicans' tolerance and even support of the January 6 coup.

Sanderson also highlights the 2018 scandal in which seven current and former students in Dartmouth College's Department of Psychological and Brain Sciences sued three faculty members for engaging in sexual harassment and assault for more than sixteen years; Dartmouth settled the case for $14 million the following year. Leah Somerville, a former graduate student at Dartmouth who is now a Harvard psychology professor, described how she gradually got used to such behavior: "If you are steeped in an environment with toxic norms, it is

likely that you can't even see it for yourself. For example, while I was there it was common for certain faculty members to joke about details of trainees' sex lives in the lab and public settings. At first, this made me very uncomfortable. But as those types of exchanges happened regularly and became more egregious, they seemed less and less scandalous."[21] In all types of settings, we are less likely to notice and act on unethical behavior when it occurs gradually, on a slippery slope—and more likely to become complicit.

Fear

About a decade ago, I was teaching negotiation for a U.S.-based multinational corporation in an Asian country whose democracy had emerged from a dictatorship in recent years. My negotiation classes are highly interactive, and I depend on the interesting insights and stories of students to improve the class and get my points across. In this particular course, however, I was having a tough time getting the students to speak up. So, to encourage their participation, I resorted to cold-calling on them. That strategy was even less well received than pure lecturing; when a student did respond, they typically used as few words as possible. All in all, I found it to be a very difficult teaching assignment.

As the course ended, the student who spoke English most fluently, as a result of living in the United States for a couple of years, approached me and offered insights I wished I'd had at the beginning of the class. She explained that during the era of dictatorship, no one wanted to stick out, as doing so was dangerous. Raising one's hand in class was a form of sticking out. So, when I called on someone, their learned behavior was to get out of focus as quickly as possible. While the dictatorship

had ended, the fear of sticking out in a classroom generalized from when the students had attended high school and college during authoritarian rule. Never having had encountered such fright in my classroom, I was stunned.

I hope that these students had nothing to fear from participating in my class. Nonetheless, they had learned a fear response from similar environments in the past. In many of the profiles covered in this book, avoiding complicity means incurring some real risk, and fear is a reasonable emotional response to that risk. This is particularly true in our discussion of authority and loyalty. If observers are receiving cues that speaking out against authority would be dangerous, it is easy to imagine them overgeneralizing that fear to contexts where safe means of speaking out exist. We may simply learn a fear response that keeps us from taking action to avoid complicity.

As we noted in chapter 6, Ronan Farrow found in his reporting that few in the entertainment industry dared to cross Harvey Weinstein. "One phone call and you're done," Weinstein repeatedly warned employees.[22] After seeing how distraught women were after "meetings" with Weinstein, one of the assistants who arranged them, Michelle Franklin, told Weinstein she wouldn't participate anymore. She was soon fired. And according to Dennis Rice, Miramax's president of marketing in the late 1990s and early 2000s, he'd seen his boss touch women inappropriately and then pay them off. "They were encouraged to not make this a big deal, otherwise their career may end," he said.[23] Weinstein enforced a "code of silence" by requiring employees to sign contracts promising they would not speak out against him or the company.

As this story shows, fear of retaliation for speaking up can be fully rational. In other cases, however, people might overgeneralize their fear to contexts where it is not warranted.

In addition, they might worry that they will face retaliation not only from the wrongdoer but also from other complicitors or observers. They may fear spending too many personal resources on speaking out or worry that they won't be believed or will be slandered. They may also fear losing their privilege if ethical changes occur.

Now What?

This chapter has overviewed just a few of the psychological mechanisms that help to explain our complicity. This list is far from complete. We also know that people often are unsure about how to respond when they witness wrongdoing. The question of how to intervene effectively—outing the bad behavior without being punished for speaking up—can be baffling. As a result, people often hide from the problem, hoping it will go away on its own or be reported by someone else. It's easy to have empathy for those who may lack the skills and knowledge needed to avoid complicity and confront wrongdoing. In chapter 10, I offer advice to help all of us confront our own complicity. And in chapter 11, we look at ways to help others avoid becoming complicit in the first place.

10

Confronting Our Own Complicity

"In the end, we will remember not the words of our enemies but the silence of our friends."
—DR. MARTIN LUTHER KING JR. (*THE TRUMPET OF CONSCIENCE*, 1967)

In 2016, near the end of President Obama's term in office, Erica Newland took a job as an attorney-adviser in the Office of Legal Counsel of the U.S. Department of Justice. Twenty-nine years old and a recent Yale Law School graduate, she had clerked for federal judge Merrick Garland (whom President Obama nominated to the Supreme Court and President Biden appointed as U.S. attorney general when he took office). Newland had decided to pursue a career in the public interest rather than cashing in on her valuable education by joining a large corporate law firm, writes George Packer in the *Atlantic*.[1] The Office of Legal Counsel was responsible for providing nonpartisan assessments of whether particular presidential executive orders

and other executive actions were lawful. Newland was a civil libertarian who believed in constraints on presidential power, and her hiring suggested that the Obama Justice Department was open to alternative views, according to Packer.

After Donald Trump was elected president in 2016, Newland decided to stay at her job. Though she expected her new bosses to be wary of her as an Obama carryover, she hoped to build a career as a government lawyer. She also believed she would play a valuable role by scrutinizing Trump's policies more closely than whomever the administration might replace her with if she resigned.

Just days after Trump's inauguration, the new acting head of the Office of Legal Counsel, Curtis Gannon, approved Trump's hastily enacted ban on visitors from seven majority-Muslim countries, a decision that threw U.S. airports into chaos and outraged many with its blatant racism and callousness. Newland, who was not involved in the matter, decided to stay on the job, even as many of her colleagues began to quit.

During Trump's second year as president, Newland and other lawyers at the Office of Legal Counsel grew fearful. Their new boss, Assistant Attorney General Steven Engel, was a Trump loyalist who tended to make unilateral decisions rather than consulting staff lawyers. In addition, the policies the office was being asked to justify increasingly involved limiting the rights of noncitizens. Lawyers in the office "began to shut up," Packer reports.[2] When Newland asked colleagues in the lunch-room what they thought of a White House press release that used the word "animals" ten times to describe members of Central American gangs, they grew uneasy and clammed up. They were aware of the risk of being fired and potentially becoming the target of an irate tweet from Trump. Career officials "saw what was happening to colleagues in the FBI who had crossed

the president during the investigation into Russian election interference—careers and reputations in ruins," Packer writes.

One of Newland's superiors took to saying, "We're just following orders." When Newland, who is Jewish, reacted to one such statement with a look, her boss added, "I know that's what the Nazis said, but we're not Nazis." Newland responded that the president himself had called some white supremacists "very fine people." Her supervisor didn't deny it but noted that he, Engel, and Attorney General Jeff Sessions had never said such a thing.

Newland began to hate her job. She believed that rather than providing a defense against egregiously racist and legally shaky policies, she and her colleagues were "using their legal skills to launder [Trump's] false statements" and arguments to allow them to "pass constitutional muster," writes Packer.[3] She also felt that she and other career attorneys were being used to legitimize repugnant policies, including the Muslim ban. Still, she worried that if she left, whoever replaced her would make things even worse. Newland wondered what kind of government lawyer she would have been if she had held her job in Germany in the 1930s—a zealot, an opportunist, a resister from the inside? She concluded that she would have done her best to tone down Hitler's racist laws but eventually would have fled.

In October 2018, a white supremacist opened fire in a Pittsburgh synagogue, killing eleven people. Online, the killer had blamed Jews for enabling Mexicans to enter the United States. Newland concluded that the work being done in her office "was sanctioning rhetoric that had inspired a mass killer," writes Packer.[4] Three days after the shooting, she quit. She soon joined the nonprofit Protect Democracy, which fights for free, fair, and fully informed self-government.

In a *New York Times* editorial published after Trump lost reelection, Newland wrote about how the Office of Legal

Counsel eroded to become complicit with evil.[5] According to her, Trump created a culture of fear throughout the federal government in which people he deemed insufficiently loyal would be fired. That fear kept people from speaking out about the injustice, malfeasance, and illegal behavior they witnessed.

In the editorial, published about two weeks before the January 6, 2021, attack on the Capitol by Trump supporters, Newland apologized for her collaboration and described her descent into complicity:

> I never harbored delusions about a Trump presidency. Mr. Trump readily volunteered that his agenda was to disassemble our democracy, but I made a choice to stay at the Justice Department—home to some of the country's finest lawyers—for as long as I could bear it. I believed that I could better serve our country by pushing back from within than by keeping my hands clean.[6]

That belief was misplaced, she concludes:

> No matter our intentions, we were complicit. We collectively perpetuated an anti-democratic leader by conforming to his assault on reality. We may have been victims of the system, but we were also its instruments. No matter how much any one of us pushed back from within, we did so as members of a professional class of government lawyers who enabled an assault on our democracy—an assault that nearly ended it.

Ultimately, Newland concludes that if she and other Justice Department attorneys had collectively refused to participate in Trump's systematic attacks on our democracy from the beginning, his efforts would have failed. "In giving voice to those trying to destroy the rule of law and dignifying their efforts

with our talents and even our basic competence, we enabled that destruction," she writes. "Were we doing enough good elsewhere to counterbalance the harm we facilitated, the way a public health official might accommodate the president on the margins to push forward on vaccine development? No."

I admire Newland for going public about her complicity, and I believe her honesty and self-criticism should inspire all of us to explore how we may be complicit in allowing others to do harm. As I read Newland's reflections, I thought about where I had drawn my own ethical lines in my own career. In the years prior to Trump's 2016 election, I worked for and gave talks at many U.S. government agencies, including the Department of Justice, the Federal Trade Commission (FTC), the Securities and Exchange Commission, the Public Company Account-ing Oversight Board (which provides oversight of corporate accounting activities in the United States), and multiple areas of the military and intelligence communities. As Trump transi-tioned into office, I was in the middle of serving as an expert wit-ness for the FTC in its suit against pharmaceutical firms accused of conspiring to keep prices high by preventing generics from coming to the market. I strongly believed that my work for the FTC was on the right side of justice. At the same time, I despised Trump for his bullying, lying, cheating, and racism; his many alleged assaults against women; and his ignorance. I feared the damage he would do while in office, and I did not at all like the idea of working for his administration. I concluded that it would be irresponsible of me to leave in the middle of the case, since I believed my work was creating net good. However, I resolved not to accept any additional work for the U.S. government as long as Trump was in power. But did staying on the case make me complicit in bolstering a corrupt administration that was threatening to destroy our democratic system?

In addition to giving us opportunities to look back at our own potential complicity, Newland's story can inspire us to think about how we can avoid being complicit in the future. We are all susceptible to being complicit in ways that we would not endorse for ourselves or approve of in others. But simple awareness of the potential of becoming complicit may be insufficient. We need to anticipate our potential complicity and develop explicit plans to avoid it.

One key challenge to avoiding complicity is recognizing that our decisions at critical moments will not be as ethical as those we would plan or endorse ahead of time. When what would be instrumentally best for us conflicts with the most ethical action we could take, we often are more likely to plan to be ethical than to actually be ethical in the moment of decision.[7] Ample research shows that virtuous choices are more prevalent when we think about a behavior in the future and that more instrumental concerns tend to dominate when it is actually time for action. For example, people are more likely to make charitable donations and support investment in long-term environmental issues if the cost of such prosocial behaviors is in the future rather than in the present.[8] For this reason, the time to think about our complicity is now, not when we are facing an important moral dilemma.

Action Steps

The following action steps offer advice on how to prepare to be courageous, deliberative, inclusive, persistent, effective, and less complicit. None of these steps will fit every opportunity we have to avoid complicity. One's status in a given situation may well affect the degree to which these ideas are viable. But I hope that thinking about these action steps will provide you with more options.

Reduce the risk of speaking up. Speaking up can be danger-ous and scary. Not everyone is in a position to speak up, but there may be steps we can take to reduce the risk of doing so and allow many to take that risk to avoid complicity. If you're facing a moral dilemma at work, one strategy that may reduce the risk of speaking up and increase your ability to act ethically would be to develop an appealing alternative to your current job so that you would be comfortable with the idea of losing it if you speak up. Negotiation scholars note that a strong source of power in negotiation is one's ability to walk away and pur-sue another option. For this reason, we advise negotiators to develop their Best Alternative to a Negotiated Agreement, or BATNA, before they begin to negotiate and to continue to revise their BATNA as negotiations continue.[9] Similarly, when it comes to avoiding complicity, having a fine alternative to your current job should provide you with the comfort and power needed to encourage ethical action.

What if you love your job and don't want to lose it? You can also make it difficult for your superiors to punish you for speaking up by increasing your value to the organization. In a *Harvard Business Review* article, management scholar James Detert notes that when you're a highly valued team member, your colleagues will be more tolerant of your views and more willing to listen if you speak out about wrongdoing to avoid complicity.[10] Notably, this may mean choosing our battles, writes Detert. Being constantly critical about infractions will make you less credible when important actions are needed to avoid complicity with evil. To reduce the risk that the wrong-doer will successfully deny your account, you should also be sure to document any questionable incidents you observe.

Finally, you can reduce the risk of speaking up by team-ing up with other colleagues who want to do the right thing.

By comparing notes with coworkers, you might gain further evidence to support and confirm your hunches. In one of the most famous early experiments in social psychology, Solomon Asch found that his male study participants knowingly gave wrong answers in a quiz a majority of the time in order to conform with the consensus view of the group to which they had been assigned.[11] But when at least one member of their group gave accurate answers, the study participants were much less likely to conform to the clearly incorrect judgments of other members. The results suggest that being around just one accurate and honest partner can dramatically improve our behavior. Plus, when it comes time to speak up, you are more likely to be heard and taken seriously when you come forward with others, and less likely to be ignored or punished.

Deliberate in advance. As noted above, we tend to overestimate the extent to which we will choose the most ethical action at the time of a decision. When we are planning our future actions, we engage our cognition, which leads us toward more ethical behaviors than our intuition would.[12] By contrast, in the moment of decision, our emotions and intuitive System 1 thinking tend to take over. Selfish motivations, fear of punishment, and tribalism grow stronger and make us more likely to become complicit.

As we have seen, uncertainty about whether someone has committed wrongdoing typically inspires complacency. Instead, it should motivate you to try to find out more. Approaching situations more deliberatively, using System 2 thinking, can help us avoid being fooled by the types of false prophets we learned about in chapter 5. When people ask us to suppress our deliberation, we should immediately be suspect.

In addition to doing your research, you can also make commitments to yourself about the person you want to be,[13]

including establishing conditions in which you will choose to act ethically rather than becoming complicit. You might also want to spend some time thinking about your personal moral code. For example, you could study a moral values framework—such as Jonathan Haidt's, which we discussed in chapter 6—and consider which values are most important to you.[14] As we saw in chapter 9, thinking through values and scenarios in advance increases the likelihood that we will reject and confront unethical behavior.

Acknowledge your blind spots. We can all do a better job of recognizing some of the ordinary tendencies toward complicity that affect most of us. By recognizing the complexity of the situations in which we find ourselves, we can avoid single sourcing of blame, looking beyond the immediate wrongdoer to consider who else may be culpable. We also need to accept that we may be just as morally culpable for our inaction as for our action and that we have a moral responsibility to speak up when we see wrongdoing. In addition, we can aim to recognize that we are less likely to notice and act on unethical behavior when it occurs gradually, over time. With this awareness in mind, we may become more attuned to subtle shifts in others' behavior and take time to consider if it is ethical and legal. Finally, when serving in the role of adviser, we need to pause to consider if our advice might harm others. If so, we need to accept responsibility for any possible ill effects rather than emphasizing that our advisee's final decision is not ours.

Enlarge the circle. In chapter 6, I presented Peter Singer's argument that the most ethical decisions tend to encompass the largest group of people possible.[15] In contrast, when we focus narrowly on our own group—such as our employer, our family, our church, or some other group to which we belong—we may end up helping that group at the expense of other parties or

society as a whole. In the process, we act in ways that are complicit with wrongdoing. As we enlarge our circle of concern, Singer highlights, we move toward taking actions that create the greatest collective good. Enlarging our circle of concern can also help those of us who belong to privileged groups see our privilege more clearly and try more actively to be equitable toward those who have less privilege. To reduce our complicity with our inequitable society, we may need to sacrifice some of our own privilege to help build a more level playing field.

By reducing the risks to speaking up, deliberating more in advance, recognizing our blind spots, and enlarging our circle of concern, we can reduce the likelihood of being complicit and move toward great ethicality. Such action steps are evident in the profiles that follow.

You Can Avoid Complicity: Profiles of Positive Action

This section provides a brief tour of people who avoided complicity in some very interesting ways, sometimes incurring significant costs in the process. From their stories, we can gain the courage needed to avoid complicity.

A survivor speaks out. In a January 2018 social media post, superstar gymnast Simone Biles revealed that she was one of the hundreds of girls and women who were sexually abused by Larry Nassar when he was the team doctor for the U.S. women's national gymnastics team, a story recounted in chapter 6. "Most of you know me as a happy, giggly, and energetic girl," Biles wrote.[16] "I've felt a bit broken and the more I try to shut off the voice in my head the louder it screams." Like many of the other abuse survivors, Biles didn't only blame Nassar for the

abuse. "No, I will not and should not carry the guilt that belongs to Larry Nassar, [USA Gymnastics], and others," she wrote.

As she came to terms with the fact that she had been abused, Biles fell into a depression, sleeping a lot because it "was like the closest thing to death for me at that point."[17] While slowly recovering, with the help of therapy, she began to recognize the power of her words. Three days after Biles tweeted that U.S. national team gymnasts shouldn't have to train at the center in Texas where Nassar molested so many girls, USAG broke ties with the center. And the CEO of USAG was fired after Biles criticized her for expressing disapproval of NFL quarterback Colin Kaepernick's decision to kneel during the national anthem.[18]

Many other survivors of Nassar's abuse have also spoken out forcefully against his complicitors, but as the "Greatest of All Time" in her sport, Biles's statements may have a unique power to effect change. In a *Today* show interview, she said one of the main reasons she decided to train for the 2020 Olympics at age twenty-four, despite dealing with tremendous physical pain, was to keep pressure on USAG and the U.S. Olympic and Paralympic Committee (USOPC) to reform: "I just feel like everything that happened, I had to come back to the sport to be a voice, to have change happen. If there weren't a remaining survivor in the sport, they would've just brushed it to the side."[19] Beyond Nassar's crimes, Biles began using her platform to hold others accountable for injustice; she supported the Black Lives Matter movement and other causes. After Nike was criticized for penalizing its sponsored female athletes financially when they became pregnant, Biles switched her endorsement contract from Nike to women's clothing company Athleta, a company that she said aligned with her values.[20]

Speaking to reporters before the U.S Gymnastics Championships in August 2019, Biles, with tears in her eyes, held USAG

officials accountable for allowing Nassar's abuse to continue for years. "We had one job," she said, "and we have done everything that they asked us for—even when we didn't want to. And they couldn't do one damn job! You had one job; you literally had one job, and you couldn't protect us!"[21] She concluded, "The people I had known for years had failed us."

A year later, while traveling to Indianapolis for a mandatory U.S. women's gymnastics training camp, Biles criticized USAG's latest proposal for settling hundreds of lawsuits filed by survivors, which would release USAG and USOPC officials, former coaches, and others from liability. The proposal failed to meet survivors' key demand that USAG disclose who concealed Nassar's abuse. And it offered a $215 million payout to more than 500 litigants, less than half the amount Michigan State University agreed to pay 332 litigants. "Ugh at the airport," Biles tweeted. "Still want answers from USAG and USOPC. Wish they BOTH wanted an independent investigation as much as the survivors & I do. Anxiety high."[22]

As the Olympics got underway in Tokyo in 2021, exactly six years after the first civil lawsuit was filed against Nassar, USAG still had not managed to reach settlements with the survivors—including Biles. In an interview with the *Times* before the Olympics, Biles made it clear who she was competing for—and who she wasn't: "I'm going to go out there and represent the U.S.A., represent World Champions Centre, and represent Black and brown girls over the world. At the end of the day, I'm not representing U.S.A. Gymnastics."[23]

"I truly do feel like I have the weight of the world on my shoulders at times," Biles wrote on Instagram after her qualifications performance at the Olympics.[24] During the team competition, she became dangerously disoriented during a vault and decided to withdraw, fearing she could be seriously

injured, though she returned to win a bronze medal on the balance beam. "I have to focus on my mental health," she later explained.[25] When asked whether the lingering trauma of Nassar's abuse affected her at the Olympics, she responded, "Now that I think of it, maybe in the back of my head, probably yes, because there are certain triggers."[26] Testifying to a Senate committee on September 15, 2021, with three other gymnasts whom Nassar had abused, Biles said, "To be clear, I blame Larry Nassar, but I also blame an entire system that enabled and perpetrated his abuse."[27] USAG and USOPC reached a $380 million settlement with Biles and more than five hundred other survivors three months later. Since the Olympics, Biles has been noncommittal about when she will retire from her sport, but there is no doubt she will continue to speak up to hold complicitors accountable for wrongdoing, in gymnastics and beyond.

Two votes to impeach. In his 1956 book, *Profiles in Courage*, President John F. Kennedy describes brave acts by eight U.S. senators. Kennedy, then the junior senator from Massachusetts, argued in the Pulitzer Prize–winning book that senators have a craving to be liked. They want to "get along with our fellow legislators, our fellow members of the club, to abide by the clubhouse rules and patterns, not to pursue a unique and independent course which would embarrass or irritate the other members," particularly members of their own party, according to Kennedy.[28] Further, he writes, "some Senators tend to take the easier, less troublesome path to harmonize or rationalize what at first appears to be a conflict between their conscience— or the result of their deliberations—and the majority opinion of their constituents." The eight senators profiled in *Profiles in Courage* pursued a more difficult path and avoided complicity. Decades later, so did Republican senator Mitt Romney.

I don't share many of Senator Romney's political views. I also love dogs and am deeply committed to reducing animal suffering. So when I read that Romney put his dog in a (custom) cargo container on the roof of his car so that the human Romney family members would be more comfortable on a road trip, that pretty much eliminated him as someone whom I would endorse as a model human being. Nevertheless, I agree that he was an excellent candidate for the John F. Kennedy Profile in Courage Award, which he won in 2021.[29]

In February 2020, with President Donald Trump standing trial for impeachment for withholding congressionally authorized military aid from Ukraine for his own political gain, Romney became the first senator in U.S. history to vote to remove a president of his own party from office. In a speech on the Senate floor just before the vote, Romney said he could not "disregard what I believe my oath and the Constitution demands of me for the sake of a partisan end."[30] "The president asked a foreign government to investigate his political rival," Romney said. "The president withheld vital military funds from that government to press it to do so. The president delayed funds for an American ally at war with Russian invaders. The president's purpose was personal and political. Accordingly, the president is guilty of an appalling abuse of the public trust."[31] Romney said he was aware that many in his party, including the president, would disapprove of his decision and denounce him. "Does anyone seriously believe I would consent to these consequences other than from an inescapable conviction that my oath before God demanded it of me?"[32] he said. In an interview with the *New York Times* before the vote, Romney conveyed an understanding of the lengths to which humans can go to deny their complicity with wrongdoing when they have incentives to do so: "I have found, in business in particular but also in

politics, that when something is in your personal best interests, the ability of the mind to rationalize that that's the right thing is really quite extraordinary. I have seen it in others, and I have seen it in myself."[33]

A year later, after Trump lost the 2020 presidential election, many Republicans escalated their complicity beyond my cynical expectations to cast doubt on the legitimacy of the election. Once again, Romney acted with courage, defending the integrity of the election and strongly opposing efforts by members of his party to overturn the Electoral College results. On January 6, 2021, after the attempted coup by Trump supporters at the U.S. Capitol, Romney called on his fellow Republican senators to tell the truth about Trump's loss. And when Trump was again on trial for impeachment, this time for inciting insurrection, Romney was one of six Republican senators to vote to convict him.

"Senator Romney's commitment to our Constitution makes him a worthy successor to the senators who inspired my father to write *Profiles in Courage*," said Caroline Kennedy, the late president's daughter, in a statement from the JFK Library Foundation. "He reminds us that our Democracy depends on the courage, conscience and character of our elected officials."[34] I agree, and I view Romney as a role model for those of us who wish to avoid complicity in our own lives.

A whistleblower who made tapes. Many parties have been blamed for the Great Recession that started in late 2007 and stretched into 2009. One of these parties was investment bank Goldman Sachs, which marketed complex mortgage securities without telling consumers that the investments were very risky and that Goldman was betting that the investments' value would fall. This conflict of interest should have been reviewed by the Federal Reserve (Fed), a 2011 Senate investigation of the recession concluded.[35]

The Fed is responsible for regulating and supervising banks and the banking system in the United States. While the agency is broadly charged with acting in the public interest, the actual history and content of Fed rules and policy tend to reflect the interests of its most powerful political and financial stakeholders.[36] Many have argued that the Fed is subject to "regulatory capture," a phenomenon that occurs when regulatory agencies come to be dominated by the industries or interests they are charged with regulating. Regulatory capture can come about through the close working relationships that regulators develop with those they regulate, especially when regulators hope to be employed by the companies they are overseeing. As a result of regulatory capture, an agency charged with acting in the public interest instead acts in ways that benefit the firms being regulated.

In a confidential report that the New York Fed (a branch of the U.S. Federal Reserve) commissioned after the financial crisis, Columbia University professor David Beim blamed regulatory capture for the Fed's failure to identify the warning signs of the financial crisis. Fed regulators were too risk averse and deferential to the banks they were regulating, and Fed employees feared speaking up and contradicting their superiors, he concluded.[37] To prevent another crisis, Beim believed, the Fed would need to change its culture. He recommended that the New York Fed hire "out-of-the-box thinkers" and "disruptive personalities" who would be unafraid to speak up about any red flags they observed at the banks they were examining.[38]

Following Beim's advice, the New York Fed hired new examiners as the country was recovering from the recession. One of them was Carmen Segarra, a forty-one-year-old lawyer who was raised primarily in Puerto Rico; studied at Cornell, Columbia, and Harvard; and worked in compliance for thirteen years. Outspoken, principled, and direct, Segarra "appeared to

be exactly what Beim ordered," according to an investigative account of the Fed's inner workings by ProPublica and NPR.[39]

After coming on board in October 2011, Segarra was assigned to the Fed team in charge of regulating Goldman Sachs. Right away, she was so alarmed by her boss's and coworkers' timidity toward Goldman Sachs, and by their criticism of her for raising concerns, that she secretly began recording her conversations with Fed officials and with Goldman executives. Notably, the head of the New York Fed, William Dudley, had worked for Goldman for twenty-one years, and Goldman's chairperson, E. Gerald Corrigan, was the ex-head of the New York Fed.[40] Two months into her time at the Fed, Segarra grew frustrated when Michael Silva, who led the New York Fed relationship team examining Goldman Sachs, failed to push the bank hard about a deal it was doing with a Spanish bank, Banco Santander, that he thought was "legal but shady." In the aftermath of the recession, the European Banking Authority had increased the amount of capital that banks were required to hold to cover any potential losses. To circumvent this requirement, Santander reduced its required capital by transferring assets to Goldman's Brazilian subsidiary. Goldman contracted to receive $40 million for holding these assets for a few years—a transaction that Silva described as "getting paid to watch a briefcase."[41]

Segarra also examined Goldman while it was advising natural gas transmission company El Paso Corporation in its negotiation to potentially be acquired by energy infrastructure company Kinder Morgan. The negotiation made headlines when a judge rebuked Goldman for having a $4 billion stake in Kinder Morgan, an obvious conflict of interest that it did not disclose to its client, El Paso. In addition, a shareholder lawsuit alleged that the top Goldman Sachs banker involved in advising El Paso held a $340,000 personal stake in Kinder Morgan.[42]

In her review of the El Paso engagement, Segarra asked to see Goldman's conflict-of-interest policy and evidence that it had properly disclosed its conflict of interest to El Paso and Kinder Morgan.[43] The Fed requires banks to have companywide conflict-of-interest policies and to avoid taking on clear-cut cases of conflict of interest that materially affect their clients. Segarra—who had spent years writing company conflict-of-interest policies in the private sector—concluded not only that Goldman had no firmwide policy but also that Goldman instructed employees not to write down anything about conflicts of interest in emails or other written communications.[44]

Segarra wrote in a draft report for the Fed that Goldman Sachs did not have a companywide conflict-of-interest policy. In a conversation she recorded, Michael Silva pressured her to tone down her criticism of the bank and say only that it needed to improve its existing policies. She repeatedly refused. A week later, Silva fired Segarra. Segarra unsuccessfully sued the Fed; the husband of the judge who heard the case was a Goldman adviser. When Segarra's attorney asked the judge about her husband's relationship with Goldman, the judge accused the Segarra team of "judge shopping." In September 2014, Segarra released audio recordings of over forty-six hours of meetings with her colleagues at the Fed, which formed the basis of the exposé by *This American Life* and ProPublica.[45]

"What do we need to effectively reform the financial system?" asks journalist Jan Weir in an article for Rantt Media. "We need a hundred Carmen Segarra's."[46] I agree. She too can inspire those of us who strive to avoid complicity with wrongdoing.

Exposing Theranos's fraud. Chapter 5 described the complicit roles that Walgreens executives and the Theranos board, including board member and former secretary of state George Shultz, played in the rise of the fraudulent company.

As I mentioned, Shultz's grandson Tyler Shultz, an entry-level Theranos employee, came to believe that Holmes and others at the company were concealing the fact that the company's technology didn't work. So did Tyler's friend and colleague Erika Cheung.

"Since when did $2+2=6$?" Cheung asked herself when she realized Theranos was cherry-picking data to make the technology appear accurate.[47] When she raised concerns within the company, Theranos COO Sunny Balwani and others tried to lead her to believe that she "was the crazy one." Tyler Shultz describes an episode in which he and a number of coworkers tested their own blood for syphilis using Theranos technology. The fact that "a ton of us tested positive" told Shultz that the equipment was not ready for the market. When he reported the results, his lab manager shrugged and said, "Guys, it's not impossible."[48]

Theranos founder Elizabeth Holmes and COO Sunny Balwani created a culture of secrecy and fear within the company. "It was just sort of instilled in us in our onboarding," Cheung said. "We need to keep certain things secret. You're not allowed to talk to friends and family about what's going on here." Employees were scared of upsetting Holmes and Balwani and losing their jobs. She elaborated: "When things would go wrong, everyone was looking to point to someone to blame."[49]

The longer he was at Theranos, the more Tyler Shultz realized that the impressive results Holmes had presented to his grandfather weren't living up to the hype. He and Cheung privately compared notes and reached similar conclusions. In March 2014, Tyler used a pseudonym to contact the Clinical Laboratory Evaluation Program of the New York State Department of Health, which ran a testing program in which Theranos participated. In emails to the program's director, without using the company's name, Tyler described practices

he'd witnessed at Theranos. The director confirmed that such practices were a form of "cheating" that would violate federal and state requirements.

Tyler filed an anonymous complaint against Theranos with New York State's Laboratory Investigative Unit. He also told his grandfather that Theranos performed the majority of the blood tests it was hired to run on other companies' equipment. Holmes's public claims about Theranos were simply not true, he said, and he was planning to quit. George Shultz urged Tyler to speak with Holmes first, though he had already done so, and she'd brushed him off.

Tyler sent Holmes a long email summarizing his concerns. Several days later, Balwani replied with an angry email dismissing Tyler's objection point by point. Tyler responded by quitting. He was asked to leave the same day. As he was on his way to his car, his mother called and begged him, "Stop whatever you're about to do!" Holmes had just phoned George Shultz and "told him that if you [Tyler] insist on carrying out your vendetta against her, you will lose," his mother said.[50] Tyler drove to his grandfather's office and shared his email to Holmes and Balwani's reply. George Shultz told his grandson that he thought he was wrong about Theranos, then invited him over for dinner that night to further discuss the matter.

Meanwhile, Balwani went through Tyler's emails and found out that Cheung had shared confidential information with him. Balwani summoned Cheung to his office and berated her. "You need to tell me if you want to work here or not," he said at the end of their meeting.[51]

That night, Cheung joined Tyler for dinner at his grandfather's house, and the two elaborated on their claims. Standing firmly with Elizabeth Holmes, George Shultz continued to

insist that the young employees didn't understand Theranos's technology. Cheung and Tyler left the dinner feeling frustrated. Cheung quit the next day.

In early 2015, Tyler confidentially shared the story of his time at Theranos as well as key documents with *Wall Street Journal* reporter John Carreyrou. When Carreyrou sent a detailed email to Theranos outlining topics he wanted to discuss with Holmes, Theranos officials deduced that he had been talking to Tyler Shultz. At George Shultz's house, two lawyers representing Theranos (from the firm Boies, Schiller & Flexner, which also engaged in aggressive tactics while defending Harvey Weinstein) ambushed Tyler, threatening to sue him if he didn't sign a paper affirming that he would honor his confidentiality agreement with the company. Though Tyler's parents and grandfather urged him to sign, Tyler stood firm.

In his first *Wall Street Journal* exposé of Theranos, published on October 15, 2015, Carreyrou raised questions about the accuracy of the company's medical devices and noted the danger to patients, drawing on his interviews with Tyler Shultz. The article triggered widespread scrutiny of the company and marked the beginning of its public downfall. By helping to expose the fraudulent behavior at Theranos, Tyler Shultz and Erika Cheung likely saved lives.

While George Shultz remained loyal to Team Theranos for a very long and unacceptable period of time, when the evidence of fraud became undeniable, he was able to update his opinion of Tyler:

> The members of our family work to be loyal and supportive to one another and to the best of America's values. Most have inspired others to listen to their better angels; and some

have shown tremendous courage and integrity when faced with difficult decisions or situations. Tyler's handling of the troubling practices he identified at Theranos is an example. He did not shrink from what he saw as his responsibility to the truth and patient safety, even when he felt personally threatened and believed that I had placed allegiance to the company over allegiance to higher values and our family. I have learned—from my experiences beginning in World War II, in private industry, and in the various public service positions I have been privileged to fill—that the people in the field are closest to the issues and are the best sources of wisdom whenever a problem arises. That was certainly the case here. Tyler navigated a very complex situation in ways that made me proud. He has been an example for the entire family, for which all of us are grateful. I want to recognize and congratulate Tyler for his great moral character.[52]

In addition to serving as an inspiring story of employees who fought off the complicity that infected so many of their coworkers, the story of Erika Cheung and Tyler Shultz also highlights the isolation that people often experience when confronted with wrongdoing. As noted earlier, teaming up with one or more partners is one way to develop the courage needed to avoid complicity.

Cheung and Shultz's partnership also parallels multiple stories behind the discovery of scientific fraud. In my earlier book *The Power of Noticing*, I described the discoveries of fraudulent data produced separately by two prominent psychologists, Harvard professor Marc D. Hauser and Tilberg University professor Diederik Stapel, slightly more than a decade ago.[53] In each story, the wrongdoing was discovered when multiple junior colleagues shared their suspicions and took their concerns to

their universities collectively. In chapter 11, we will look at what leaders can do to make the ethical journey for less powerful employees an easier pathway in their organizations.

Saving millions of people from the harms of tobacco. Getting people to not smoke cigarettes remains one of the most important public health strategies worldwide. Tobacco killed about one hundred million people in the twentieth century and will kill far more in the twenty-first century.[54] The fact that tobacco causes lung cancer was known by the early 1950s, but this scientific evidence was hidden from the public due to extensive advertising and lobbying efforts by the tobacco industry.[55] For many decades, the industry worked to sow false doubt about the health hazards of smoking. Stanford historian Robert Proctor coined the term "agnotology" to describe the intentional production of ignorance (as opposed to knowledge) and cited the tactics of the tobacco industry as a prime example.[56] Today we talk about fake news, but the tobacco industry spread misinformation for decades.

Many were complicit with the tobacco industry, including physicians. As the medical community slowly learned about the harms of smoking, from the 1920s to the 1960s, the tobacco industry had a strong ally in the American Medical Association (AMA). When the U.S. surgeon general released a report in 1964 highlighting the hazards of smoking, the AMA helped the industry tamp down its influence. The AMA refused to acknowledge the harms caused by tobacco because it didn't want to alienate legislators from tobacco-growing states. At the time, the AMA was more concerned about pending legislation to create Medicare and Medicaid, programs it perceived as threats to doctors' earnings. Big Tobacco's strategies, combined with the complicity of thousands of its employees and strange partners, like the AMA, slowed the potential for

regulatory reform through the rest of the century. It wasn't until the 1990s that the industry's fake-news strategy began to collapse.

One fascinating person in the story of this collapse was Jeffrey Wigand. As the very well-paid vice president of research and development at the U.S. tobacco company Brown & Williamson (B&W), Wigand was charged with finding safer ways to deliver nicotine to consumers, including reducing the harm caused by other chemical compounds in cigarettes. His research also examined "impact boosting," or enhancing nicotine absorption so that it would affect the brain and nervous system faster. Wigand believed impact boosting marked a deliberate attempt to increase addiction. He was also concerned about coumarin, a carcinogenic tobacco additive that B&W used as a flavor enhancer, which Wigand described as "a form of rat poison."[57] B&W consistently ignored Wigand's recommendations for reducing the addictiveness and carcinogenic properties of its products. After Wigand got into a disagreement with B&W's CEO, Thomas Sandefur, he was fired.

Wigand signed a confidentiality agreement that prohibited him from saying anything about his work with B&W. Nonetheless, in a 1995 interview with the CBS show *60 Minutes*, he claimed that Sandefur told him that his research "would clearly expose every other product as being unsafe and, therefore, present a liability issue."[58] Interestingly, under pressure from B&W, which reportedly threatened to sue the network for its role in Wigand's decision to violate his nondisclosure agreement, CBS didn't air the interview until a year later, after the *Wall Street Journal* broke Wigand's story.[59] CBS was complicit with Big Tobacco during this time, just as NBC was complicit in Harvey Weinstein's crimes years later when it succumbed to his threats and refused to air Ronan Farrow's reporting on the scandal.

By going public, Wigand played a significant role in the changes that started to take place at the end of the century, including constraints on advertising by the tobacco industry, limits on where people can smoke, and tougher enforcement to keep minors from having access to cigarettes. These changes contributed to the reduction in smoking that we have seen in the last quarter century. In 1998, the U.S. tobacco industry agreed to pay a $368 billion settlement to forty-six states for its advertising and marketing of cigarettes. In his new career, Wigand consults on tobacco-control policies with governments all over the world.

Obviously, there were many other heroes in the fight to reduce deaths caused by cigarettes. But Wigand stands out for refusing to become complicit in his organization's actions and violating his confidentiality agreement to help save lives.

Many Republicans other than Romney had the courage to stand up to Trump, and there are many corporate whistle-blowers other than Segarra, Tyler Shultz, Cheung, and Wigand. Unfortunately, however, they remain a small minority among a much larger group of complicitors. Too many employees accept wrongdoing within their organization and become complicit, and too many leaders allow their organizations to develop cultures that enable and encourage complicity. Those in leadership positions need to consider the behavior their organization currently encourages and find ways to prompt more ethical behavior. That is where we are headed next.

11

Leading Broader Solutions to Complicity

On September 6, 2021, as I was completing the first draft of this book, I received an email from a former Harvard graduate student. This individual did not take a course from me but had heard me speak on behavioral economics at the Center for Public Leadership in the Harvard Kennedy School of Government, and he now owned and ran a chain of restaurants. He was interested in making his restaurants safer from COVID-19 transmission during the surge of the highly contagious Delta variant, a goal that was easy to admire. "We would like to encourage our employees to get vaccines," he wrote. "Our COO suggested that we pay our employees $100 for the Johnson and Johnson or $50 per shot for the other two part vaccines. . . . We are discussing this tomorrow, but I was curious to reach out to you, per your presentation . . . to ask if you have suggestions/recommendations, best practices from behavioral economics or even heuristics that we should use to help preemptively keep more [of] our employees and their families safe in terms of vaccines or consistent mask usage."

I wanted to help this individual achieve his goals and was happy that he asked me to think about his role as a leader who could potentially influence his employees and the health of his customers. But I was bothered by the assumption in the email that he was thinking about nudging or motivating behavior rather than mandating it. "Thanks for moving in the right direction," I wrote. "However, my honest view is that the only ethically responsible policy for a food service company is to mandate vaccinations (with verification) as a condition of employment. I certainly would not want to go to a restaurant with unvaccinated personnel. And, failure to make vaccination mandatory would, in my view, make you complicit in any cases of COVID spread in your restaurant. Sorry to be harsh—but my ethical views are clear on this." I then answered his exact question, responding, "In the interest of equity, and based on the social science of norm creation, I would recommend incentives based on 100% vaccination by groups—e.g., specific locations, and let the vaccinated do the communication work for you." I closed the email apologizing for what might be perceived as my harshness.

My view was clearly influenced by the utilitarian perspective that we have a moral obligation to maximize welfare for all. I fully recognized that others place unique value on individual freedoms. Yet, in the case of COVID, allowing customer-facing employees to be unvaccinated imposes costs on customers that I believe society should find unacceptable. How do we balance the freedom of people to choose not to vaccinate themselves versus the freedom of customers to not be exposed to COVID? My answer comes from thinking about the policy that maximizes value across all people. More value is created by allowing vaccinated people to live their lives with lower risk of catching COVID, being hospitalized, or dying from the disease than

from allowing unvaccinated people to move about freely with a much higher risk of being infected and infecting others.

I still read my email as harsh, yet I stand by my response. Leaders are privileged in many ways; they often accrue prestige, respect, and wealth from their position. They also accrue a broader ethical mandate. Leaders have abundant opportunities to affect the ethics of others for the better. When they fail to use that opportunity, they may be complicit in any harm that results. Thus, one reason my message to this leader was blunt was that I felt if I failed to offer my honest option, I would have been complicit in any COVID-19 transmission that occurred in his restaurants as a result of the lack of a vaccination mandate. I was relieved when the restaurateur responded pleasantly, writing, "I receive your advice here and do not find it to be harsh, I deeply appreciate your commitment to have the highest expectations of me here."

In chapter 10, we considered what we can do as individuals to avoid being complicit with others' wrongdoing in the future. But as is evident in the restaurant story and in many of the stories we've discussed throughout the book, individual actors are only part of the equation. At Theranos and WeWork, managers, top company leaders, investors, and board members went along with the founders' deception. In the stories involving the Trump administration, powerful people who knew better enabled his corruption and supported his lies. Many people at Miramax, The Weinstein Company, and other organizations helped Harvey Weinstein assault women again and again. And as we saw, top leaders in the Catholic Church, USA Gymnastics, the U.S. Olympic Committee, Michigan State, Penn State, and numerous other organizations allowed serial abusers to remain in positions where they could continue to assault people.

Clearly, if so many leaders, groups of employees, organizations, and government bodies can become complicit in wrongdoing, there is also much they can do to reduce the likelihood of complicit behavior in their organizations. Many of us are leaders, whether of our families, communities, organizations, or government entities. Leaders are different from other professionals in that they are responsible not only for their own decisions but also for the decisions of those they lead.[1] Thus, leaders who seek to avoid being complicit with harm need to think about not just their own decisions, but the decisions of those around them. Moving beyond the question of how to reduce our own complicity, in this chapter we will think about what leaders can do to reduce complicity by others through the use of groups, the design of their organizations, and the creation of institutions that reduce wrongdoing in society at large.

Leaders influence whether followers care about ethicality and justice, or instead prioritize authority and loyalty—or, in the case of some religious organizations, sanctity. While some leaders duck responsibility and deny their complicity in the unethical actions of organizational members, other leaders think about why their members behave as they do and develop wise solutions to encourage ethical behavior and reduce complicity. It can be difficult, if not impossible, to prevent true evildoers from trying to commit harm. But there *are* clear steps we can take to stop the ordinary people around them from enabling and participating in their behavior. In this chapter, we explore ways that those with the privilege and responsibility associated with being a leader might work toward creating a more responsible organization by prompting others to be less complicit in wrongdoing.

Empowering Group Action

In the closing days of the Trump administration, top leaders in the U.S. Department of Justice (DOJ) were stunned to learn that the president had devised a plan to oust acting attorney general Jeffrey A. Rosen and then use the power of the DOJ to force the state of Georgia to overturn its presidential election results in Trump's favor.[2] Trump came up with this plot after Rosen refused to carry out the president's plan to corrupt the election results. Upon learning of the plot, DOJ leaders had a choice to make. They could stand by and allow the corruption to take place. They could simply resign, in which case it might happen anyway. Instead, they made an informal pact, agreeing that if Rosen were fired, they would resign as a group. This threat of group action persuaded Trump to keep Rosen in place. He recognized that mass resignations by so many top DOJ leaders would create an uproar that would work against his ongoing baseless accusations of voter fraud.[3] The group of DOJ leaders recognized that together, they had the power to avoid being complicit that no single one of them had alone.

Around the same time that DOJ leaders were using their group power to avoid complicity, a leadership team within the U.S. Census Bureau was struggling to keep that organization apolitical and honest. Every decade since 1790, the U.S. government has attempted to count all of the country's residents to determine a fair distribution of federal funds and allocation of congressional seats to the fifty states. By law, the census "must be independent from political and other undue external influence in developing, producing, and disseminating statistics."[4] For centuries, the census has been largely successful at meeting that goal of nonpartisanship—at least, until Trump came along.

On July 21, 2020, just months before the election, Trump directed the U.S. Department of Commerce to instruct the Census Bureau, which it oversees, to estimate the number of undocumented immigrants in its 2020 population count and subtract this number from its total.[5] Doing so would have favored Republican-leaning states in the allocation of seats in Congress and Electoral College votes. The many legal rulings that followed went against Trump. After all, the Constitution specifies that all "persons" living in states—not just voters or citizens—are supposed to be included in the census.[6]

With the clock running down on his presidency, Trump ordered his political appointees at the Census Bureau, including its director, Steve Dillingham, to tabulate undocumented immigrants separately from citizens and legal permanent residents, and to eliminate the undocumented from the count. Because the census does not ask residents about their immigration status, identifying those who lack documents is a very difficult task that is bound to be inaccurate. But Trump demanded a best estimate from Dillingham.

Dillingham and other recent Trump appointees couldn't do this on their own; they needed help from experienced career employees at the bureau. In their efforts, they tried to enlist three experts, who had a combined record of seventy-five years of experience at the Census Bureau and a shared reputation for nonpartisanship: John Abowd, the bureau's chief scientist; Tori Velkoff, the chief demographer; and deputy director Ron Jarmin. Together, these three leaders agreed to refuse to meet Dillingham's demand unless they would be allowed to explain in a technical report why their estimates of undocumented immigrants were useless—which would have publicly invalidated the information.[7] This collective action allowed the leaders to run out the clock until Trump was no longer president,

when the 2020 census data became safe from political abuse. Abowd, Velkoff, and Jarmin could not have held the line on their own; they needed to work together.

These incidents at government agencies during the Trump administration show the powerful role of group action in confronting and blocking wrongdoing. In chapter 10, we saw how Tyler Shultz and Erika Cheung teamed up to avoid complicity at Theranos and help put an end to Holmes's fraud, as well as how graduate students have partnered to expose academic scandals. Sometimes employees who are trying to prevent wrongdoing and avoid complicity come together by chance. But leaders also have the potential to create mechanisms that encourage organizational members to band together to stop unethical action. Too many organizations do just the opposite, creating cults of secrecy.

Designing a Moral Organization

Too many people, including leaders, view the design and structure of their organization as relatively fixed. But people created the organization, and leaders have the power to change key features of it.[8] By thinking about how their organization is set up, leaders can identify why employees might act in ways that enable unethical conduct.

Harvard Business School professor Michael Tushman and Stanford professor Charles O'Reilly offer a model of organizational design, known as the congruence model, that can be used to diagnose why organizations act the way they do and to identify how leaders can move the organization closer to its goals.[9] According to Tushman and O'Reilly, leaders can better understand behavior within their organization by studying four aspects of the organization's design: (1) the critical

tasks facing the organization; (2) how the organization's culture encourages some behaviors and not others; (3) how the organization is organized, in terms of its hierarchy and informal communication channels; and (4) the nature of those who are selected into and promoted by the organization. By examining whether these four components clash or are congruent, leaders can move their organization toward better performance, Tushman and O'Reilly write.

This model also offers a way of promoting more ethical behavior. By thinking about each of these components, leaders can identify not only why some members might be acting in unethical ways but also why those around them may be enabling their unethical behavior, including bribes, theft, favoritism to in-groups, and financial manipulation. Leaders can use the congruence model to audit their organization by assessing what Tushman and O'Reilly refer to as the performance gap, or the difference between an organization's actual performance and the performance that leaders seek. For our purposes, the congruence model can help leaders think through how to reduce complicity with unethical behavior in their organizations.

Many universities experience a performance gap between the level of sexual harassment and assault that exists on their campuses as compared to their goal of having no harassment or assault at all. To meet the critical task of creating a campus environment where everyone can feel safe and be safe, what has to change? The congruence framework would encourage us to think about what cultural norms the organization espouses, the nature of the organizational structure that might affect desired behavior, and who belongs to the organization. With this in mind, university leaders can assess what behaviors its culture normalizes. They can determine whether reporting structures allow information to flow where it needs to be to stop sexual

assaults and hold perpetrators accountable. And leaders can audit whether they are doing all they can to keep sexual predators from joining and remaining in the community.

By thinking about the environment they wish to create, leaders can also identify barriers to their preferred outcomes and devise solutions. There are at least two important, unique features confronting universities regarding sexual assault. First, repeat offenders carry out the majority of assaults; second, victims are often reluctant to report assaults. Reporting to an organization where one has been sexually assaulted can be a confusing, intimidating, embarrassing, and lonely experience. And the culture and structure of most universities does little to help potential and actual victims.

Creative thinking can be used to identify unique solutions to the performance gap that most universities face on the issue of sexual assault. Legal scholars Ian Ayres and Cait Unkovic have suggested one means of empowering students and employees to come forward when they are harassed or assaulted: information escrows.[10] While emphasizing that information escrows can be structured in different ways, Ayres and Unkovic offer an example in the context of an allegation of sexual harassment: "Allow a victim to place a private complaint into escrow with instructions that the complaint be lodged with the proper authorities only if the escrow agent receives at least one additional allegation against the same individual."[11] The idea is that once two different victims of the same perpetrator enter their claim into the escrow, both can come forward without the risk of being alone. Each victim will know that the essence of their claim will be independently supported and validated by another party. Information escrows have been implemented on many college campuses as a means of responding to the fears of victims of sexual assault.

Jessica Ladd created a nonprofit organization called Callisto, which operationalizes information escrows on a digital platform to help people anonymously report sexual assaults. Callisto allows university students and others to make a time-stamped report of a sexual assault on an encrypted digital platform. Assault survivors can still choose to report their accusation to their organization and/or the police, or they can decide that Callisto should report their incident only if another person names the same perpetrator. Callisto gives survivors an opportunity to report the crime soon after it happens, which increases the likelihood that their claim will be taken seriously if it is unveiled at a later date. As I write this paragraph, over a dozen universities have adopted Callisto, and its use is growing fast in the venture capital industry and beyond.

You may have qualms regarding information escrows in the context of sexual harassment and assault. Clearly, keeping an allegation secret allows the perpetrator to go free and commit more crimes—though, in terms of accountability, reporting secretly is an improvement on not reporting at all. For our purposes, information escrows can more broadly inspire leaders to think about how to create a reporting system that will lead employees away from complicity with various types of unethical behavior.

There are all sorts of ways in which leaders can change their organization's design to try to reduce complicity. One of my favorite examples comes from one of my consulting clients (a large company that prefers to remain anonymous), whose leaders take pride in encouraging employees to do the right thing. They created a widely viewed internal video in which four senior executives each tell the story of a time when they went around their boss to alert the organization to malfeasance. The purpose of the video was to make it clear that the organization

values ethical action over respect for hierarchy. Top leaders are striving to create a culture in which members understand that the company's mission statement is a policy to be acted on rather than just a document aimed at meeting some external review standard.

Creating a More Just Society

Leaders also have a moral responsibility to increase diversity in their organizations. Finding ways for more voices and perspectives to be heard not only makes good business sense but also reduces the complicity of those in the majority in perpetuating inequity. This is beginning to happen at the School for International Studies (recently renamed the Boerum Hill School for International Studies), the New York school we learned about in chapter 4. As you'll recall, SIS had a tumultuous 2015–16 school year after a sudden influx of white students and parents. At the end of the year, a new principal, Nicole Lanzillatto, took over.[12] Concerned that SIS was losing its diversity, she reserved 40 percent of school enrollment for kids in the free or reduced-price lunch program, most of whom are kids of color. She also cut back the French program, hired more teachers and staff of color, and worked to create a school culture where equity is a key goal.

I am trying to do more to increase diversity in the organizations I belong to. As I described in chapter 4, I was disappointed when the highly qualified candidate I nominated to the Academy of Management Fellows Group was passed over, which led me to notice (too late) the group's overwhelming racial homogeneity. By the time these events developed, I was writing this book on complicity and trying my best to avoid being complicit in all areas of my life. So, with the help of some wise friends who know more than I do about improving

diversity and inclusion efforts (Dolly Chugh, Modupe Akinola, Mahzarin Banaji, and Arthur Brief), I drafted a letter encouraging the Fellows to review our processes for adding new members and solicited signatures from a total of twenty-six Fellows.

On April 23, 2021, Brief and I, both Fellows, sent a letter to the "Dean" of the Fellows expressing our view that diversity should be reflected in the selection process of new members of the Fellows Group of the academy. We noted that there was only one Black Fellow in the group, despite the many worthy candidates available, and suggested that the current nomination process could be contributing to the homogeneity. We asked the Dean to organize a "discussion of diversity among the Fellows, perhaps with outside social science experts who could advise on a wise process."

We recommended that the discussion cover the following questions:

1. Should we collect and share demographic data on the Fellows and on the membership of the broader Academy of Management?
2. Should we explicitly encourage members to actively consider candidates from underrepresented groups when nominating and voting on potential Fellows?
3. Should we empower and encourage the nominating committee to nominate candidates itself, with one goal being to create a more inclusive Fellows Group?
4. Should we allow nominations to come from outside of the current Fellows membership?

The leaders of the Fellows Group invited Fellows to attend a September 2021 Zoom meeting to discuss the nomination process. Most of the twenty-plus Fellows who attended strongly favored changing the system to improve diversity and offered

compelling reasons for doing so, while a few saw nothing wrong with the existing system.

The majority in favor of changes to improve the diversity of this honorific society supported the first three recommendations above and pushed the leadership to create a committee to make a more formal recommendation of the overall membership. The fourth recommendation had less support, either because of the added administrative complexity or because existing Fellows would have less control over the process. I am confident that positive changes are in the works and that the diversity of the Fellows will increase as a result. Again, only a few Fellows actively lobbied against increasing our diversity. For many years, most of us were simply complicit in accepting our privilege and biases in passing out honors in our profession. To enact similar changes in your organization, you can collect and study demographic data to see what improvements are needed and identify strategies to make sure that candidates from underrepresented groups are given fair consideration.

Creating Ethical Institutions

In many cases, the solution to reducing complicity and harm goes beyond a specific organization to encompass industrywide or even societywide structures. This book has documented how so many institutions have let us down, from the auditing industry, which fails to provide independent audits of public companies, to the credit-rating agencies, which offer biased ratings aimed primarily at pleasing the client, to the Federal Reserve Board being captured by the banks it is supposed to regulate. These failed structures were not created by nature or a higher being; they were created by humans in positions of

leadership who fell short of building organizations, institutions, and systems that would prevent unethical conduct.

We need to be on the lookout for failed solutions that provide an excuse for parties not to take stronger action. For example, a great deal of research provides convincing evidence that disclosure of conflicts of interest is a misdirection that is more likely to make matters worse than to make them better. That is, when health-care professionals disclose a conflict of interest, they actually feel freer to choose actions consistent with their own self-interest, simply because they disclosed it. Moreover, the recipient of the biased advice will trust the adviser more than they would have otherwise, since the adviser was nice enough to disclose the conflict of interest.[13] This research provides an important insight for creating effective policy. Policymakers often falsely assume that disclosure will solve a problem much more than it actually will. And when they falsely assume that disclosure is sufficient to resolve a conflict of interest, they no longer see the true need for the systemic change that is likely to be much more effective.

Sometimes complicitors are held accountable for tolerating or enabling wrongdoers. For example, Penn State president Graham Spanier was fired, convicted of child endangerment, and made to serve two months in prison for his complicity in the child sexual abuse committed by assistant Penn State football coach Jerry Sandusky. However, too many complicitors are held blameless by their organization, their industry, and the state, or receive a mere slap on the wrist. Few of those who enabled Harvey Weinstein, Elizabeth Holmes, Adam Neumann, or Larry Nasser have been held fully accountable for their action or inaction.

University of Utah law professor Amos Guiora, whose writing on complicity we explored in chapter 6, argues for

criminalizing complicity, at least in the content of sexual assault.[14] In doing so, he distinguishes between two types of complicitors who facilitate sexual predators: bystanders and enablers. He defines a bystander as someone who is physically present at the time of the crime and chooses not to try to stop it, such as someone who doesn't call 911 or try to restrain an attacker. In contrast, the enabler in Guiora's conceptualization learns of an assault after it takes place, due to their position in an organization, and fails to take sufficient action to help the survivor or to prevent future assaults by the same perpetrator. While enablers and bystanders are complicit in sexual assault in different ways, both typically demonstrate a failure to act, notes Guiora. As I documented in chapter 9, people are less likely to punish a violation of omission than a violation of commission.

Regarding the complicity of bystanders, Guiora notes in his 2020 book *Armies of Enablers* that ten U.S. states—California, Florida, Hawaii, Massachusetts, Minnesota, Ohio, Rhode Island, Vermont, Washington, and Wisconsin—have mandatory-reporting laws.[15] These laws vary by state on whether they apply to all crimes, apply only to attacks on children, or are focused specifically on sexual assault. When Utah was considering passing mandatory-reporting legislation, Guiora writes, some legislators opposed it for various reasons, including being against legislating morality, not wanting to create a "nanny state," or distrust of law enforcement. Focusing on the perspective of the person in peril, Guiora views those who prevent legislation to criminalize inaction by bystanders as complicit in future harms.

Because enablers usually have more time to deliberate and often more power, Guiora is far harsher on them than he is on bystanders. He writes about enablers who have access to convincing evidence of many sexual assaults by the same

perpetrator, well beyond the threshold of the information-escrow systems we described earlier, yet fail to act. These enablers typically have important positions in respected institutions, such that victims have the right to expect these leaders to help them and work to stop future crimes. When leaders in the Catholic Church, Penn State, and Michigan State failed to act, they effectively tolerated and institutionalized the criminal behavior of predators. Guiora argues that the failure to prosecute Boston archbishop Bernard F. Law much earlier, in particular, highlights the limitations of our current legal system and how valuing sanctity over justice can lead to enormous suffering. He also points out the moral failure that occurs when loyalty to an institution leads to tolerance of sexual assault. In the United States, the Child Abuse Prevention and Treatment Act requires states to enact laws mandating the reporting of abuse regardless of whether the enabler was present to witness it. But states have implemented and enforced this law in very different ways—and often insufficiently, according to Guiora.

I am convinced by Guiora's arguments that society should move toward criminalizing bystander inaction and institutional enablers. As an organizational scholar and behavioral ethicist, I add that leaders often build organizations that make unethical behavior commonplace and encourage complicity by others. Paralleling the moral obligations of lawmakers, organizational leaders need to understand that their obligations go beyond individual responsibility; they must work to identify how to reduce complicit behavior in their organizations. While Guiora focuses on the domain of sexual assault, leaders should be thinking about complicity across a broader array of possible unethical actions that occur within organizations, including deception, theft, and discrimination.

In 1863, the U.S. Congress passed the False Claims Act, sometimes called the Lincoln Law, to combat fraud against the government and its troops during the Civil War, specifically by Union Army defense contractors. To this day, the act allows people unaffiliated with the federal government to file a claim against federal contractors they believe have directly or indirectly defrauded the government. Moreover, under the act, whistleblowers who expose such cases are granted a percentage of the funds that the government recovers, thus giving citizens a strong incentive to take the risks involved in reporting fraud. This very early piece of legislation encouraged citizens to become whistleblowers.

Whistleblowers are people who provide evidence of illegal activity, gross negligence by management, abuse of authority, or a substantial and specific danger to public health or safety, according to the Government Accountability Project.[16] If someone in your organization reported the unethical conduct of others, what would happen to them? More broadly, does your organization reward or punish whistleblowers? The unfortunate truth is that, across history, whistleblowers generally have not been treated well. When potential whistleblowers can bring useful knowledge to the organization, yet are discouraged from doing so or fear being punished for speaking up, leaders are failing an ethical challenge. Not only are they encouraging complicit behavior by others, but they are themselves complicit.

Just as the False Claims Act institutionalized a process for reducing complicity at the national level, organizational leaders have an obligation to find ways to encourage employees to speak up about unethical behavior. Those in power, the organization's culture, and the systems and incentives that are in place can encourage organizational members to become whistleblowers.

Breaking the Ice

One concern I have when telling stories about unethical behavior that has occurred in organizations is that there are many fine people working in these organizations. Undoubtedly, many of these good people have already suffered from their association with unethical behavior that occurred at their workplace. Many did nothing wrong. Others did not commit wrongdoing but were complicit in the unethical behavior of others. Being complicit doesn't necessarily make one a bad human being. But we should all be motivated to want to avoid future complicity.

As I was completing this book, I was hiking with a friend, a former executive at a well-known financial firm, and told him about this book on complicity. He then told me about an episode in which he was part of a senior management team reviewing employees. One of the employees being reviewed had fine performance on many standard metrics, but there were also many reports of him harassing more junior female colleagues. As the group was closing in on a positive assessment, my friend asked whether they should be concerned about the harassment reports. As soon as the topic came up, the others in the room felt free to unload their concerns about the employee as well, and the group collectively decided to address the harassment. The message my friend took away from the episode was how simple it can be for leaders to avoid complicity. His colleagues just needed someone to break the ice.

Leaders have a special burden and opportunity to confront complicity and work to reduce it in others. Will you help initiate the changes that are needed? "Never doubt that a small group of thoughtful, committed citizens can change the world; indeed, it's the only thing that ever has," Margaret Mead has been quoted as saying.[17] This inspiring quote highlights the opportunities

and responsibilities that all of us possess to make the world a better place. Those who have the privilege of leadership must not simply accept the world as it is, but take steps to prevent wrongdoing, including by helping those they lead avoid complicity. With awareness and courage, leaders can create less complicit, more effective organizations.

Epilogue

The profiles of complicity that have formed the core of this book, along with the discussion of the psychology of complicity in chapter 9, highlight why so many of us are complicit in wrongdoing. I doubt that *Complicit* will do much to change the behavior of true partners and collaborators in evil. But I hope it will move many of us away from our ordinary complicity, which keeps us from thinking about our role in others' harm, toward more deliberative consideration of the opportunities we have to create a more ethical world. Across multiple personal examples, I have tried to highlight the degree to which we are able to make the world a slightly better place by reducing our own complicity.

In my 2014 book *The Power of Noticing*, I argued that we often fail to act on ambiguous information.[1] Ambiguity is often one of the first hints that something is wrong. As I noted earlier, multiple journalists have told me that they find the best news stories after noticing that the available data doesn't make sense. Returning to the data fraud story from chapter 7, when I first saw the insurance-company data for the field experiment, there were pieces that did not make sense to me. This should have motivated me to do more. My failure to do so made me complicit in allowing fraudulent data to be published in a highly

respected research journal and to influence organizational decisions.

I hope that if I had had access in 2011 to the knowledge I have now about complicity that I would have done more to stop the publication of a paper with fraudulent data. The data fraud story offers a final message for avoiding complicity: When something is wrong, we must not accept the easiest explanation. We need to be persistent until we fully understand what is going on. Sometimes this puts our relationships at risk. Sometimes it will be uncomfortable. But it's the ethical thing to do.

NOTES

Chapter 1

1. P. Whoriskey and C. Rowland, "McKinsey, Advisor to Businesses around the World, Agrees to Pay $573.9 Million to Settle Charges for Its Role in Opioid Epidemic," *Washington Post*, February 4, 2021, https://www.washingtonpost.com/business/2021/02/04/mckinsey-opioid-settlement-purdue/.

2. The People of the State of California v. McKinsey & Company, Inc., United States (February 4, 2021), Complaint for Permanent Injunction and Other Relief, https://oag.ca.gov/system/files/attachments/press-docs/People%20v%20McKinsey%20File%20Stamped%20Complaint.pdf.

3. I. MacDougall, "McKinsey Never Told the FDA It Was Working for Opioid Makers While Also Working for the Agency," ProPublica, October 4, 2021, https://www.propublica.org/article/mckinsey-never-told-the-fda-it-was-working-for-opioid-makers-while-also-working-for-the-agency.

4. E. Markey, "Markey Joins Senators Hassan, Grassley, and Whitehouse in Call to FDA to Provide Answers on Potential Conflicts of Interest with Consulting Firm McKinsey in Relation to Opioid Crisis," press release, August 24, 2021, https://www.markey.senate.gov/news/press-releases/markey-joins-senators-hassan-grassley-and-whitehouse-in-call-to-fda-to-provide-answers-on-potential-conflicts-of-interest-with-consulting-firm-mckinsey-in-relation-to-opioid-crisis.

5. MacDougall, "McKinsey Never Told the FDA."

6. M. Forsythe and W. Bogdanich, "McKinsey Settles for Nearly $600 Million over Role in Opioid Crisis," *New York Times*, October 27, 2021, https://www.nytimes.com/2021/02/03/business/mckinsey-opioids-settlement.html.

7. Whoriskey and Rowland, "McKinsey, Advisor to Businesses."

8. C. Clark, "McKinsey's Business Model Is Unethical," Medium, November 30, 2020, https://calebclark.medium.com/mckinseys-business-model-is-unethical-f3356a32e1fa.

9. G. Mulvihill, "McKinsey & Company Agrees to Pay Nearly $600 Million Over Opioid Crisis," PBS NewsHour, February 4, 2021, https://www.pbs.org/newshour/economy/mckinsey-company-agrees-to-pay-nearly-600-million-over-opioid-crisis.

10. Whoriskey and Rowland, "McKinsey, Advisor to Businesses."

11. Forsythe and Bogdanich, "McKinsey Settles."

12. N. Oreskes and E. M. Conway, *Merchants of Doubt: How a Handful of Scientists Obscured the Truth on Issues from Tobacco Smoke to Global Warming*, 2nd ed. (New York: Bloomsbury Press, 2020).

13. P. Singer, *Practical Ethics*, 3rd ed. (Cambridge: Cambridge University Press, 2011); M. H. Bazerman, *Better, Not Perfect: A Realist's Guide to Maximum Sustainable Goodness* (New York: Harper Business, 2020).

14. M. H. Bazerman and A. E. Tenbrunsel, *Blind Spots: Why We Fail to Do What's Right and What to Do about It* (Princeton, NJ: Princeton University Press, 2011).

15. M. R. Banaji and A. G. Greenwald, *Blindspot: Hidden Biases of Good People* (New York: Delacorte Press, 2013).

16. M. Bazerman and D. Chugh, "Decisions without Blinders," *Harvard Business Review*, January 2006, 88–97.

17. T. Aquinas, *The summa theologica* (Claremont, CA: Coyote Canyon Press, 2018).

18. C. Kutz, *Complicity* (Cambridge, UK: Cambridge University Press, 2000).

19. G. Mellema, *Complicity and Moral Accountability* (Notre Dame, IN: University of Notre Dame Press, 2016).

20. Bazerman, *Better, Not Perfect*.

21. Bazerman, *Better, Not Perfect*.

22. Banaji and Greenwald, *Blindspot*.

Chapter 2

1. U.S. Centers for Disease Control and Prevention, Opioid Overdose: Overview, https://www.cdc.gov/drugoverdose/data/prescribing/overview.html.

2. Associated Press, "White House: True Cost of Opioid Epidemic Tops $500 Billion," CNBC, November 20, 2017, https://www.cnbc.com/2017/11/20/white-house-true-cost-of-opioid-epidemic-tops-500-billion.html.

3. B. Meier, *Pain Killer: An Empire of Deceit and the Origin of America's Opioid Epidemic* (New York: Random House, 2018).

4. A. W. D. Aoyama, "The Two Arthur Sacklers," *Harvard Crimson*, October 17, 2019, https://www.thecrimson.com/article/2019/10/17/two-arthur-sacklers/.

5. G. S. Hava, "Arthur Sackler and a Victim's Legacy," *Harvard Crimson*, November 11, 2020, https://www.thecrimson.com/column/for-sale/article/2020/11/16/hava-sackler-and-victim-legacy/.

6. A. Van Zee, "The Promotion and Marketing of OxyContin: Commercial Triumph, Public Health Tragedy," *American Journal of Public Health* 99, no. 2 (2009): 221–27.

7. Meier, *Pain Killer*, 32.

8. Meier, *Pain Killer*, 75.

9. Meier, *Pain Killer*, 75.

10. E. Helmore, "Purdue Pharma Escaped Serious Charges over Opioid in 2006, Memo Shows," *Guardian*, August 10, 2020, https://www.theguardian.com/us-news/2020/aug/19/purdue-pharma-oxycontin-justice-department-memo-opioid.

11. Helmore, "Purdue Pharma."

12. Meier, *Pain Killer*, 185.

13. J. Hoffman, "Sacklers and Purdue Pharma Reach New Deal with States over Opioids," *New York Times*, March 3, 2022, https://www.nytimes.com/2022/03/03/health/sacklers-purdue-oxycontin-settlement.html?smid=em-share.

14. E. Eyre, *Death in Mud Lick: A Coal Country Fight against the Drug Companies That Delivered the Opioid Epidemic* (New York: Scribner, 2020).

15. Eyre, *Death in Mud Lick*, 5–6.

16. Eyre, *Death in Mud Lick*.

17. J. Hoffman, "CVS, Walgreens and Walmart Fueled Opioid Crisis, Jury Finds," *New York Times*, November 23, 2021, https://www.nytimes.com/2021/11/23/health/walmart-cvs-opioid-lawsuit-verdict.html.

18. "Perpetrators, Collaborators, and Bystanders," The Holocaust, https://www.holocaust.com.au/the-facts/perpetrators-collaborators-and-bystanders/.

19. J. Wolfreys, "How France's Vichy Regime Became Hitler's Willing Collaborators," *Jacobin*, July 10, 2010, https://www.jacobinmag.com/2020/07/vichy-france-holocaust-nazi-hitler-world-war-ii.

20. "MS *St. Louis*," Wikipedia, https://en.wikipedia.org/wiki/MS_St._Louis.

21. M. Kranish, "Trump Has Referred to His Wharton Degree as 'Super Genius Stuff.' An Admissions Officer Recalls It Differently," *Washington Post*, July 8, 2019, https://www.washingtonpost.com/politics/trump-who-often-boasts-of-his-wharton-degree-says-he-was-admitted-to-the-hardest-school-to-get-into-the-college-official-who-reviewed-his-application-recalls-it-differently/2019/07/08/0a4eb414-977a-11e9-830a-21b9b36b64ad_story.html; S. Eder and D. Philipps, "Donald Trump's Draft Deferments: Four for College, One for Bad Feet," *New York Times*, August 6, 2016, https://www.nytimes.com/2016/08/02/us/politics/donald-trump-draft-record.html; R. Buettner, S. Craig, and D. Barstow, "11 Takeaways from the Times's Investigation into Trump's Wealth," *New York Times*, October 2, 2018, https://www.nytimes.com/2018/10/02/us/politics/donald-trump-wealth-fred-trump.html.

22. A. Serwer, "The Nationalist's Delusion," *Atlantic*, November 20, 2017, https://www.theatlantic.com/politics/archive/2017/11/the-nationalists-delusion/546356/.

23. M. Kaplan, "Major Landlord Accused of Antiblack Bias in City," *New York Times*, October 16, 1973, https://www.nytimes.com/1973/10/16/archives/major-landlord-accused-of-antiblack-bias-in-city-us-accuses-major.html.

24. Serwer, "Nationalist's Delusion."

25. Serwer, "Nationalist's Delusion."

26. G. Hood, "The GOP Convention: Race, Identity, and Power," *American Renaissance*, July 26, 2016, https://www.amren.com/features/2016/07/the-gop-convention-race-identity-and-power/.

27. M. Fox, "Stephen Bannon's Uber-Right Religion Parked in the Bosom of the White House," March 9, 2017, https://www.matthewfox.org/blog/stephen-bannons-uber-right-religion-parked-in-the-bosom-of-the-white-house.

28. Fox, "Stephen Bannon's Uber-Right Religion."

Chapter 3

1. C. Duhigg, "How Venture Capitalists Are Deforming Capitalism," *New Yorker*, November 30, 2020, https://www.newyorker.com/magazine/2020/11/30/how -venture-capitalists-are-deforming-capitalism; R. Weideman, *Billion Dollar Loser: The Epic Rise and Spectacular Fall of Adam Neumann and WeWork* (New York: Little, Brown, 2020); E. Brown and M. Farrell, *The Cult of We: WeWork, Adam Neumann, and the Great Startup Delusion* (New York: Crown, 2021).

2. Duhigg, "Venture Capitalists."

3. Weideman, *Billion Dollar Loser.*

4. Weideman, *Billion Dollar Loser.*

5. Duhigg, "Venture Capitalists."

6. Duhigg, "Venture Capitalists."

7. Weideman, *Billion Dollar Loser.*

8. Weideman, *Billion Dollar Loser.* In an interview, Neumann later claimed that he answered, "smart guy" (see J. de la Merced, "'It Went to My Head: Adam Neumann Has Regrets about His Time at WeWork," *New York Times*, November 9, 2021, https://www .nytimes.com/2021/11/09/business/dealbook/adam-neumann-wework.html).

9. Weideman, *Billion Dollar Loser.*

10. Weideman, *Billion Dollar Loser.*

11. Weideman, *Billion Dollar Loser.*

12. Weideman, *Billion Dollar Loser.*

13. Duhigg, "Venture Capitalists."

14. J. Ewing, *Faster, Higher, Farther: The Volkswagen Scandal* (New York: W. W. Norton, 2017)

15. N. C. Smith and E. McCormick, "Volkswagen's Emissions Scandal: How Could It Happen?" INSEAD, 2018, https://publishing.insead.edu/case/volkswagen-scandal.

16. Bazerman, *Better, Not Perfect.*

17. J. B. Stewart, "Problems at Volkswagen Start in the Boardroom," *New York Times*, September 24, 2015, https://www.nytimes.com/2015/09/25/business /international/problems-at-volkswagen-start-in-the-boardroom.html.

18. K. Connolly, "Bribery, Brothels, Free Viagra: VW Trial Scandalises Germany," *Guardian*, January 13, 2008, https://www.theguardian.com/world/2008/jan /13/germany.automotive.

19. J. Ewing and K. Granville, "VW, BMW and Daimler Hindered Clean-Air Technology, European Regulator Says," *New York Times*, April 5, 2019, https://www.nytimes .com/2019/04/05/business/eu-collusion-bmw-vw-daimler-emissions.html.

20. A. Applebaum, "History Will Judge the Complicit," *Atlantic*, July/August 2020, https://www.theatlantic.com/magazine/archive/2020/07/trumps-collaborators /612250/.

21. T. Kopan, "McConnell: 'Obvious' Trump Doesn't Know Issues," CNN, June 10, 2016, https://www.cnn.com/2016/06/10/politics/mitch-mcconnell-donald-trump -issues/index.html.

22. Associated Press, "Mitch McConnell Has Gone Silent on Donald Trump as Senate Hangs in the Balance," CBS News, October 25, 2016, https://www.cbsnews.com/news/mitch-mcconnell-has-gone-silent-on-donald-trump-as-senate-hangs-in-balance/.

23. Applebaum, "History Will Judge."

24. G. Gass, "Graham: Trump's Immigration Plan Is 'Stupid' and 'Illegal,'" Politico, August 25, 2015, https://www.politico.com/story/2015/08/lindsey-graham-slams-donald-trump-immigration-proposal-121710.

25. J. Senior, "Good Riddance, Leader McConnell," New York Times, January 19, 2021, https://www.nytimes.com/2021/01/19/opinion/good-riddance-leader-mcconnell.html.

26. J. Mayer, "Why McConnell Dumped Trump," New Yorker, January 23, 2021, https://www.newyorker.com/magazine/2021/02/01/why-mcconnell-dumped-trump.

27. Applebaum, "History Will Judge."

28. L. Zhou, "'Our Democracy Would Enter a Death Spiral': Mitch McConnell Urges Republicans to Back the Election Results," Vox, January 6, 2020, https://www.vox.com/2021/1/6/22217204/mitch-mcconnell-trump-election-results.

29. J. Martin and M. Haberman, "McConnell Is Said to Be Pleased about Impeachment, Believing It Will Be Easier to Purge Trump from the G.O.P.," New York Times, January 12, 2021, https://www.nytimes.com/2021/01/12/us/mitch-mcconnell-trump-impeachment.html.

30. C. E. Lee, K. Welker, S. Ruhle, and D. Linzer, "Tillerson's Fury at Trump Required an Intervention from Pence," NBC News, October 4, 2017, https://www.nbcnews.com/politics/white-house/tillerson-s-fury-trump-required-intervention-pence-n806451.

31. K. Kelly and M. Haberman, "Gary Cohn, Trump's Advisor, Said to Have Drafted Resignation Letter after Charlottesville," New York Times, August 25, 2017, https://www.nytimes.com/2017/08/25/us/politics/gary-cohn-trump-charlottesville.html.

32. K. D. Tenpas, "Turnover in the Trump Administration," Brookings Institution, January 2021, https://www.brookings.edu/research/tracking-turnover-in-the-trump-administration/.

33. D. Malhotra and M. H. Bazerman, Negotiation Genius: How to Overcome Obstacles and Get Better Results at the Bargaining Table and Beyond (New York: Random House, 2007).

34. J. Gillespie and M. H. Bazerman, "Parasitic Integration," Negotiation Journal 13 (1997): 271–82.

35. Bazerman, Better, Not Perfect.

36. J. Greene, Moral Tribes: Emotion, Reason, and the Gap between Us and Them (New York: Penguin, 2013).

37. Greene, Moral Tribes.

38. A. H. Hastorf and H. Cantril, "They Saw a Game: A Case Study," Journal of Abnormal and Social Psychology 49, no. 1 (1954): 129–34.

39. Bazerman, Better, Not Perfect.

Chapter 4

1. C. Joffe-Walt, "Episode One: The Book of Statuses," July 30, 2020, in *Nice White Parents*, produced by J. Snyder, podcast, https://www.nytimes.com/2020/07/30/podcasts/nice-white-parents-serial.html.

2. A. Zimmer, "How Brownstone Brooklyn Parents Aim to Take Over a Struggling Middle School," DNAInfo, January 29, 2015, https://www.dnainfo.com/new-york/20150129/boerum-hill/brownstone-brooklyn-parents-aim-take-over-struggling-middle-school/.

3. Zimmer, "Brownstone Brooklyn Parents."

4. Joffe-Walt, "Book of Statuses."

5. Joffe-Walt, "Book of Statuses."

6. Joffe-Walt, "Book of Statuses."

7. Joffe-Walt, "Book of Statuses."

8. A. Farrow, *Complicity: How the North Promoted, Prolonged, and Profited from Slavery* (New York: Ballantine, 2006).

9. Farrow, *Complicity*, 4.

10. H. McGhee, *The Sum of Us: What Racism Costs Everyone and How We Can Prosper Together* (New York: One World, 2021).

11. D. A. Brown, *The Whiteness of Wealth: How the Tax System Impoverishes Black Americans—And How We Can Fix It* (New York: Crown, 2021).

12. McGhee, *The Sum of Us*, 276.

13. M. Bertrand and S. Mullainathan, "Are Emily and Greg More Employable than Lakisha and Jamal? A Field Experiment on Labor Market Discrimination," *American Economic Review* 94, no. 4 (2004): 991–1013.

14. K. L. Milkman, M. Akinola, and D. Chugh, "What Happens Before? A Field Experiment Exploring How Pay and Representation Differentially Shape Bias on the Pathway into Organizations," *Journal of Applied Psychology* 100, no. 6 (2015): 1678–712.

15. Unfortunately, Lee passed away in 2021; see A. Traub, "Lee Ross, Expert in Why We Misunderstand Each Other, Dies at 78," *New York Times*, June 16, 2021, https://www.nytimes.com/2021/06/16/science/lee-ross-dead.html.

16. M. H. Bazerman, G. F. Loewenstein, and S. B. White, "Reversals of Preference in Allocation Decisions: Judging an Alternative versus Choosing among Alternatives," *Administrative Science Quarterly* 37 (1992): 220–40.

17. K. A. Diekmann, S. M. Samuels, L. Ross, and M. H. Bazerman, "Self-Interest and Fairness in Problems of Resource Allocation," *Journal of Personality and Social Psychology* 72 (1997): 1061–74.

18. D. Chugh, *The Person You Mean to Be: How Good People Fight Bias* (New York: Harper Business, 2018).

19. B. J. Lucas, Z. Berry, L. M. Giurge, and D. Chugh, "A Longer Shortlist Increases the Consideration of Female Candidates in Male-Dominant Domains," *Nature Human Behavior* 5 (2021): 736–42.

20. McGhee, *The Sum of Us*.

21. D. M. Peterson and C. L. Mann, "Closing the Racial Inequality Gaps: The Economic Cost of Black Inequality in the U.S.," Citi GPS: Global Perspectives and Solutions, September 2020, https://www.citivelocity.com/citigps/closing-the-racial -inequality-gaps/.

Chapter 5

1. D. Morain, "Layton Sentenced to Life in Ryan's Death," *Los Angeles Times*, March 4, 1987, https://www.latimes.com/archives/la-xpm-1987-03-04-mn-4627-story .html.

2. Wikipedia, "Peoples Temple," accessed November 9, 2021, https://en.wikipedia .org/wiki/Peoples_Temple.

3. B. Weinstein, "Two Great Reasons to Stop Saying 'Drinking the Kool-Aid,'" *Forbes*, March 29, 2018, https://www.forbes.com/sites/bruceweinstein/2018/03/29 /two-great-reasons-to-stop-saying-i-drank-the-kool-aid/?sh=71dfc6b334e3.

4. "Ex-Aide to Jim Jones Kills Himself at News Briefing," *New York Times*, March 13, 1979, 18.

5. S. Pinker, *Enlightenment Now: The Case for Reason, Science, Humanism, and Progress* (New York: Viking, 2018).

6. J. Gunther, *Inside Europe* (New York: Harper & Brothers, 1940), 516–17, 530–32, 534–35.

7. J. Carreyrou, "Hot Startup Theranos Has Struggled with Its Blood-Test Technology," *Wall Street Journal*, October 14, 2015, https://www.wsj.com/articles/theranos -has-struggled-with-blood-tests-1444881901.

8. J. Carreyrou, *Bad Blood: Secrets and Lies in a Silicon Valley Startup* (New York: Knopf, 2018).

9. R. Abelson, "Theranos Founder Elizabeth Holmes Indicted on Fraud Charges," *New York Times*, June 15, 2018, https://www.nytimes.com/2018/06/15/health /theranos-elizabeth-holmes-fraud.html.

10. E. Griffith and E. Woo, "Elizabeth Holmes Is Found Guilty of Four Counts of Fraud," *New York Times*, January 3, 2022, https://www.nytimes.com/2022/01/03 /technology/elizabeth-holmes-guilty.html.

11. Carreyrou, *Bad Blood*.

12. Carreyrou, *Bad Blood*, 88.

13. J. Carreyrou, "Theranos Voids Two Years of Edison Blood Test Results," *Wall Street Journal*, May 18, 2016, https://www.wsj.com/articles/theranos-voids-two-years -of-edison-blood-test-results-1463616976; Carreyrou, *Bad Blood*, 289.

14. B. Unglesbee, "Walgreens Wants Court to Toss Theranos Lawsuit," Retail-Dive, May 9, 2019, https://www.retaildive.com/news/walgreens-wants-court-to-toss -theranos-lawsuit/554464/.

15. A. Edgecliffe-Johnson, "Adam Neumann, the Salesman-Guru Out to Prove That We Works," *Financial Times*, January 11, 2019, https://www.ft.com/content/20900d4c -1582-11e9-a581-4ff78404524e.

16. G. Sherman, "'You Don't Bring Bad News to the Cult Leader': Inside the Fall of WeWork," *Vanity Fair*, November 21, 2019, https://www.vanityfair.com/news/2019/11/inside-the-fall-of-wework.

17. Sherman, "Inside the Fall."

18. Sherman, "Inside the Fall."

19. Edgecliffe-Johnson, "Adam Neumann."

20. Sherman, "Inside the Fall."

21. Sherman, "Inside the Fall."

22. Sherman, "Inside the Fall."

23. Sherman, "Inside the Fall."

24. Weideman, *Billion Dollar Loser*.

25. Sherman, "Inside the Fall."

26. Wikipedia, "Cult," accessed November 9, 2021, https://en.wikipedia.org/wiki/Cult.

27. Wikipedia, "Faith and Rationality," accessed November 9, 2021, https://en.wikipedia.org/wiki/Faith_and_rationality.

28. Wikipedia, "Faith and Rationality."

29. Anonymous, "Faith and Reason in Islam," *Dawn*, July 24, 2009, https://www.dawn.com/news/844220/faith-reason-in-islam.

30. Pope John Paul II, *Fides et Ratio*, encyclical letter, Vatican website, September 14, 1998, https://www.vatican.va/content/john-paul-ii/en/encyclicals/documents/hf_jp-ii_enc_14091998_fides-et-ratio.html.

31. D. Kahneman, *Thinking, Fast and Slow* (New York: Farrar, Straus, & Giroux, 2013); Pinker, *Enlightenment Now*.

32. K. E. Stanovich and R. F. West, "Individual Difference in Reasoning: Implications for the Rationality Debate?" *Behavioral and Brain Sciences* 23, no. 5 (2000): 645–726.

33. D. Moore and M. H. Bazerman, *Decision Leadership* (New Haven, CT: Yale University Press, 2022).

Chapter 6

1. R. Farrow, "From Aggressive Overtures to Sexual Assault: Harvey Weinstein's Accusers Tell Their Stories," *New Yorker*, October 10, 2017, https://www.newyorker.com/news/news-desk/from-aggressive-overtures-to-sexual-assault-harvey-weinsteins-accusers-tell-their-stories.

2. M. Twohey, J. Kantor, S. Dominus, J. Rutenberg, and S. Eder, "Weinstein's Complicity Machine," *New York Times*, December 5, 2017, https://www.nytimes.com/interactive/2017/12/05/us/harvey-weinstein-complicity.html.

3. Twohey et al., "Weinstein's Complicity Machine."

4. Twohey et al., "Weinstein's Complicity Machine."

5. R. Farrow, *Catch and Kill: Lies, Spies, and a Conspiracy to Protect Predators* (New York: Little, Brown, 2019), 246.

6. Farrow, "Harvey's Weinstein's Accusers"; Twohey et al., "Weinstein's Complicity Machine."

7. Farrow, "Harvey's Weinstein's Accusers."

8. J. Kantor and M. Twohey, "Harvey Weinstein Paid Off Sexual Harassment Accusers for Decades," *New York Times*, October 5, 2017, https://www.nytimes.com/2017/10/05/us/harvey-weinstein-harassment-allegations.html.

9. Farrow, *Catch and Kill*, 246.

10. Farrow, *Catch and Kill*, 38–39.

11. Kantor and Twohey, "Harvey Weinstein."

12. Farrow, *Catch and Kill*, 124.

13. Twohey et al., "Weinstein's Complicity Machine."

14. Farrow, *Catch and Kill*.

15. Farrow, *Catch and Kill*, 240.

16. D. McDonald, "Sir Peter Jackson: Harvey Weinstein Made Me Blacklist Stars," *Stuff*, December 16, 2017, https://www.stuff.co.nz/entertainment/99921399/sir-peter-jackson-harvey-weinstein-made-me-blacklist-stars.

17. Farrow, *Catch and Kill*, 173.

18. Farrow, *Catch and Kill*, 155.

19. R. Farrow, "'I Haven't Exhaled in So Long': Surviving Harvey Weinstein," *New Yorker*, February 25, 2020, https://www.newyorker.com/news/q-and-a/i-havent-exhaled-in-so-long-surviving-harvey-weinstein.

20. J. Haidt, *The Righteous Mind: Why Good People Are Divided by Politics and Religion* (New York: Pantheon Books, 2012).

21. J. Barajas, "How the Nazi's Defense of 'Just Following Orders' Plays Out in the Mind," PBS NewsHour, February 20, 2016, https://www.pbs.org/newshour/science/how-the-nazis-defense-of-just-following-orders-plays-out-in-the-mind.

22. International Law Commission, "Principles of International Law Recognized in the Charter of the Nüremberg Tribunal and in the Judgment of the Tribunal, 1950," ICRC website, accessed November 9, 2021, https://ihl-databases.icrc.org/applic/ihl/ihl.nsf/Treaty.xsp?action=openDocument&documentId=854DDAACFDE285E4C12563CD002D6B95.

23. T. Evans, M. Alesia, and M. Kwiatkowski, "Former USA Gymnastics Doctor Accused of Abuse," *Indianapolis Star*, September 12, 2016, https://www.indystar.com/story/news/2016/09/12/former-usa-gymnastics-doctor-accused-abuse/89995734/.

24. "Larry Nassar Case: USA Gymnastics Doctor 'Abused 265 Girls,'" BBC News, January 31, 2018, https://www.bbc.com/news/world-us-canada-42894833.

25. E. Levenson, "Michigan State University Reaches $500 Million Settlement with Larry Nassar Victims," CNN, May 17, 2018, https://www.cnn.com/2018/05/16/us/larry-nassar-michigan-state-settlement/index.html.

26. J. Barr and D. Murphy, "Nassar Surrounded by Adults Who Enabled His Predatory Behavior," ESPN.com, January 16, 2018, https://www.espn.com/espn/otl/story/_/id/22046031/michigan-state-university-doctor-larry-nassar-surrounded-enablers-abused-athletes-espn.

27. Barr and Murphy, "Nassar Surrounded by Adults."

28. L. Clarke, "Senate Panel: Negligence by Olympic, USA Gymnastics Officials Enabled Abuse by Ex-Team Doctor Nassar," *Washington Post,* July 30, 2019, https:// www.washingtonpost.com/sports/olympics/panel-to-introduce-legislation-to-reform -us-olympic-and-paralympic-committee/2019/07/30/7472683e-b266-11e9-8f6c -7828e68cb15f_story.html.

29. L. Roscher, "Nassar Abuse Survivors Reach $380 Million Settlement with USA Gymnastics," Yahoo! Sports, December 13, 2001, https://sports.yahoo.com/nassar-survivors -reach-380-million-settlement-with-usa-gymnastics-194745758.html?guccounter=1.

30. J. Macur, "Biles and Her Teammates Rip the F.B.I. for Botching Nassar Abuse Case," *New York Times,* September 15, 2021, https://www.nytimes.com/2021/09/15 /sports/olympics/fbi-hearing-larry-nassar-biles-maroney.html?smid=em-share.

31. Macur, "Biles and Her Teammates."

32. T. Farragher, "Admission of Awareness Damning for Law," *Boston Globe,* December 14, 2002, http://www.boston.com/globe/spotlight/abuse/stories3/121402 _admission.htm.

33. Greene, *Moral Tribes.*

34. Bazerman and Tenbrunsel, *Blind Spots.*

35. A. Guiora, *The Crime of Complicity: The Bystander in the Holocaust* (Chicago: American Bar Association, 2017).

36. A. Guiora, *Armies of Enablers: Survivor Stories of Complicity and Betrayal in Sexual Assaults* (Chicago: American Bar Association, 2020).

37. J. A. Hildreth, F. Gino, and M. H. Bazerman, "Blind Loyalty? How Group Loy- alty Makes Us See Evil or Engage in It," *Organizational Behavior and Human Decision Processes* 132 (2016): 16–36.

38. A. Libson and G. Parchomovsky, "The Curse of Loyalty," working paper, March 2022.

39. D. Barrett and M. Laris, "Former Boeing Chief Test Pilot Indicted on Fraud Charge in Probe of 737 Max Crashes," *Washington Post,* October 14, 2021, https://www .washingtonpost.com/national-security/boeing-indict-mark-forkner-pilot/2021/10/14 /166e2dfc-2d3b-11ec-985d-3150f7e106b2_story.html.

40. P. Valdes-Dapena, "GM: Steps to a Recall Nightmare," CNN Money, accessed June 17, 2014, https://money.cnn.com/infographic/pf/autos/gm-recall-timeline/.

41. CBS/AP, "General Motors Announces 30th Recall of Year," CBS News, May 23, 2014, https://www.cbsnews.com/news/general-motors-announces-30th-recall-of -year/.

42. B. Vlasic, "A Fatally Flawed Switch, and a Burdened Engineer," *New York Times,* November 13, 2014, https://www.nytimes.com/2014/11/14/business/a-fatally-flawed -switch-and-a-burdened-engineer.html.

43. Vlasic, "Fatally Flawed Switch."

44. Vlasic, "Fatally Flawed Switch."

45. "VW Engineer Sentenced to 40-Month Prison Term in Diesel Case," CNBC, August 26, 2017, https://www.cnbc.com/2017/08/26/vw-engineer-sentenced-to-40 -month-prison-term-in-diesel-case.html.

46. B. Vlasic, "Volkswagen Engineer Gets Prison in Diesel Cheating Case," *New York Times*, August 25, 2017, https://www.nytimes.com/2017/08/25/business/volkswagen-engineer-prison-diesel-cheating.html.

47. E. O. Wilson, *Sociobiology: The New Synthesis* (Cambridge, MA: Harvard University Press, 1975).

48. Wilson, *Sociobiology*.

49. Singer, *Practical Ethics*.

50. Singer, *Practical Ethics*.

51. T. Arango, N. Bogel-Burroughs, and J. Senter, "3 Former Officers Are Convicted of Violating George Floyd's Civil Rights," *New York Times*, February 24, 2022, https://www.nytimes.com/2022/02/24/us/guilty-verdict-george-floyds-rights.html.

52. J. Mustian, "'I'm Scared': AP Receives Video of Deadly Arrest of Black Man," AP News, May 19, 2021, https://apnews.com/article/louisiana-arrests-monroe-eca0 21d8a54ec73598dd72b269826f7a.

53. Mustian, "AP Receives Video."

54. J. Mustian and J. Bleiberg, "Beatings, Buried Videos a Pattern at Louisiana State Police," AP News, September 8, 2021, https://apnews.com/article/police-beatings -louisiana-video-91168d2848b10df739d73cc35b0c02f8.

55. Mustian and Bleiberg, "Beatings, Buried Videos."

56. M. al-Gharbi, "Police Punish the 'Good Apples,'" *Atlantic*, July 1, 2020, https://www.theatlantic.com/ideas/archive/2020/07/what-police-departments-do-whistle -blowers/613687/.

57. al-Gharbi, "Police Punish the 'Good Apples.'"

58. al-Gharbi, "Police Punish the 'Good Apples.'"

59. GBD 2019 Police Violence U.S. Subnational Collaborators, "Fatal Police Violence by Rate and State in the USA, 1980–2019: A Network Meta-Regression," *Lancet* 398 (2021): 1239–55.

60. T. Arango and S. Dewan, "More than Half of Police Killings Are Mislabeled, New Study Says," *New York Times*, September 30, 2021, https://www.nytimes.com/2021 /09/30/us/police-killings-undercounted-study.html?referringSource=articleShare.

61. J. Haidt, *The Righteous Mind: Why Good People Are Divided by Politics and Religion* (New York: Pantheon Books, 2012).

Chapter 7

1. U. Simonsohn, J. Simmons, and L. Nelson, "Evidence of Fraud in an Influential Field Study about Dishonesty," DataColada, August 17, 2021, http://datacolada.org/98.

2. L. Shu, N. Mazar, F. Gino, D. Ariely, and M. Bazerman, "Signing at the Beginning Makes Ethics Salient and Decreases Dishonest Self-Reports in Comparison to Signing at the End," *Proceedings of the National Academy of Sciences* 109, no. 38 (2012): 15197–200.

3. I sent an earlier draft of this book chapter to all of my coauthors to check my facts for accuracy.

4. Bazerman and Tenbrunsel, *Blind Spots*.

5. Google Scholar, "Signing at the Beginning Makes Ethics Salient and Decreases Dishonest Self-Reports in Comparison to Signing at the End," accessed November 9, 2021, https://scholar.google.com/citations?view_op=view_citation&hl=en&user =NGKWT4gAAAAJ&cstart=20&pagesize=80&citation_for_view=NGKWT4g AAAAJ:3htObqc8RwsC.

6. A. S. Kristal, A. V. Whillans, M. H. Bazerman, F. Gino, L. L. Shu, N. Mazar, and D. Ariely, "Signing at the Beginning versus at the End Does Not Decrease Dishonesty," *Proceedings of the National Academy of Sciences* 117 (2020): 7103–107.

7. S. M. Lee, "A Famous Honesty Researcher Is Retracting a Study over Fake Data," BuzzFeed News, August 20, 2021, https://www.buzzfeednews.com/article /stephaniemlee/dan-ariely-honesty-study-retraction.

8. Lee, "Famous Honesty Researcher."

9. Lee, "Famous Honesty Researcher."

10. R. C. Mayer, J. H. Davis, and F. D. Schoorman, "An Integrative Model of Organizational Trust," *Academy of Management Review* 20 (1995): 709–34.

Chapter 8

1. K. R. Tringale, D. Marshall, T. K. Mackey, M. Connor, J. D. Murphy, and J. A. Hattangadi-Gluth, "Types and Distributions of Payments from Industries to Physicians in 2015," *Journal of the American Medical Association* 317, no. 17 (May 2, 2017): 1774–84.

2. A. P. Mitchell, N. U. Trivedi, R. L. Gennarelli, S. Chimonas, S. M. Tabatabai, J. Goldberg, L. A. Diaz Jr., and D. Korenstein, "Are Financial Payments from the Pharmaceutical Industry Associated with Physician Prescribing?" *Annals of Internal Medicine*, March 2021, https://www.acpjournals.org/doi/10.7326/M20-5665.

3. Mitchell et al., "Financial Payments."

4. Mitchell et al., "Financial Payments."

5. Alosa Health website, accessed November 10, 2021, https://alosahealth.org/.

6. Alosa Health website, accessed November 10, 2021, https://alosahealth.org/.

7. P. R. Lichter, "Debunking Myths in Physician-Industry Conflicts of Interest," *American Journal of Ophthalmology* 146, no. 2 (August 2008): 159–71.

8. D. Koreinstein, S. Keyhani, and J. S. Ross, "Physician Attitudes toward Industry: A View across the Specialties," *Archives of Surgery*, June 2010, https://pubmed.ncbi .nlm.nih.gov/20566978/.

9. S. P. Kim, C. P. Gross, P. L. Nguyen, M. C. Smaldone, R. H. Thompson, N. D. Shah, A. Kutikov, L. C. Han, R. J. Karnes, J. Y. Ziegenfuss, and J. S. Tilburt, "Specialty Bias in Treatment Recommendations and Quality of Life among Radiation Oncologists and Urologists for Localized Prostate Cancer," *Prostate Cancer and Prostatic Diseases* 17, no. 2 (June 2014): 163–69.

10. D. A. Myers, "Consuming Health: Physician Conflict, Patient Care, and Developing Technology," *Southern California Interdisciplinary Law Journal* 14 (2005): 151–80.

11. D. A. Moore, D. M. Cain, G. Loewenstein, and M. Bazerman, eds., *Conflicts of Interest. Problems and Solutions from Law, Medicine, and Organizational Settings* (New York: Cambridge University Press, 2005).

12. C. Grassley, "Grassley Statement on Efforts to Address Conflicts of Interest in Medicine," press release, April 1, 2009, https://www.grassley.senate.gov/news/news-releases/grassley-statement-efforts-address-conflicts-interest-medicine.

13. J. Feinman, *Delay, Deny, Defend: Why Insurance Companies Don't Pay Claims and What You Can Do about It* (New York: Portfolio, 2010).

14. Feinman, *Delay, Deny, Defend.*

15. S. Kolhatkar, "McKinsey's Work for Saudi Arabia Highlights Its History of Unsavory Entanglements," *New Yorker*, November 1, 2018, https://www.newyorker.com/news/news-desk/mckinseys-work-for-saudi-arabia-highlights-its-history-of-unsavory-entanglements.

16. Kolhatkar, "McKinsey's Work for Saudi Arabia."

17. J. Cotterill, "Global Firms Under Scrutiny in Isabel dos Santos Alleged Corruption Leak," *Financial Times*, January 20, 2020, https://www.ft.com/content/cf261ec8-3b7e-11ea-b232-000f4477fbca.

18. M. Boyle, "McKinsey Pulls Back from Russia after Staff, Alumni Assailed Firm's Stance," Bloomberg News, March 3, 2022, https://www.bloombergquint.com/onweb/mckinsey-staff-alumni-pushed-firm-to-cut-ties-to-russia-after-ukraine-invasion.

19. P. Sauer, "McKinsey Chief Admits Email Banning Staff from Attending Navalny Rally Incorrectly Reflected Policy," *Moscow Times*, January 25, 2021, https://www.themoscowtimes.com/2021/01/25/mckinsey-chief-admits-email-banning-staff-from-navalny-protest-incorrectly-reflected-firms-policy-a72722.

20. L. D. Ordóñez, M. E. Schweitzer, A. D. Galinsky, and M. H. Bazerman, "Goals Gone Wild: The Systematic Side Effects of Over-Prescribing Goal Setting," *Academy of Management Perspectives* 23, no. 1 (2009): 6–16.

21. Ordóñez et al., "Goals Gone Wild."

22. Ordóñez et al., "Goals Gone Wild."

23. M. Cheng, K. R. Subramanyam, and Y. Zhang, *Earnings Guidance and Managerial Myopia*, unpublished paper (Los Angeles: University of Southern California, 2005), https://papers.ssrn.com/sol3/papers.cfm?abstract_id=851545.

24. D. J. Simons and C. F. Chabris, "Gorillas in Our Midst: Sustained Inattentional Blindness for Dynamic Events," *Perception* 28, no. 9 (1999): 1059–74.

25. M. Schweitzer, L. Ordóñez, and B. Douma, "Goal Setting as a Motivator of Unethical Behavior," *Academy of Management Journal* 47, no. 3 (2004), 422–32.

26. Bazerman and Tenbrunsel, *Blind Spots.*

27. S. Cowley, "Wells Fargo Review Finds 1.4 Million More Suspect Accounts," *New York Times*, August 13, 2017, https://www.nytimes.com/2017/08/31/business/dealbook/wells-fargo-accounts.html.

28. B. McClean, "How Wells Fargo's Cutthroat Corporate Culture Allegedly Drove Bankers to Fraud," *Vanity Fair*, May 31, 2017, https://www.vanityfair.com/news/2017/05/wells-fargo-corporate-culture-fraud.

29. McClean, "Wells Fargo's Cutthroat Corporate Culture."

30. C. Arnold, "Former Wells Fargo Employees Describe Toxic Sales Culture, Even at HQ," National Public Radio, October 4, 2016, https://www.npr.org/2016/10/04/496508361/former-wells-fargo-employees-describetoxic-sales-culture-even-at-he.

31. B. Van Rooij and A. Fine, "Toxic Corporate Culture: Assessing Organizational Processes of Deviancy," *Administrative Science* 8 (2018): 23.

32. E. S. Reckard, "Wells Fargo's Pressure-Cooker Sales Culture Comes at a Cost," *Los Angeles Times,* December 21, 2013, https://www.latimes.com/business/la-fi-wells -fargo-sale-pressure-20131222-story.html.

33. M. Egan, "More Wells Fargo Workers Allege Retaliation for Whistleblowing," CNN, November 7, 2017, http://money.cnn.com/2017/11/06/investing/wells-fargo -retaliation-whistleblower/index.html.

34. Van Rooij and Fine, "Toxic Corporate Culture."

35. A. Lustgarten and R. Knutson, "Years of Internal BP Probes Warned That Neglect Could Lead to Accidents," ProPublica, June 7, 2010, https://www.propublica .org/article/years-of-internal bp probes-warned-that-neglect-could-lead-to-accidents.

36. L. C. Steffy, *Drowning in Oil: BP and the Reckless Pursuit of Profit* (New York: McGraw Hill Professional, 2010).

37. Van Rooij and Fine, "Toxic Corporate Culture."

38. Moore et al., *Conflicts of Interest.*

39. The last three paragraphs have been influenced by conversations I have had with Adi Libson and Yuval Feldman.

40. M. Bazerman, G. Loewenstein, and K. Morgan, "The Impossibility of Auditor Independence," *Sloan Management Review* 38, no. 4 (1997): 89–95.

41. AICPA, "Objectivity, Integrity and Disclosure," accessed November 9, 2021, https://www.aicpa.org/interestareas/personalfinancialplanning/resources/practice center/professionalresponsibilities/objectivityintegritydisclosure.html.

42. J. Swanson, "Ratings Agencies Hit for Role in Financial Crisis," Mortgage News Daily, October 22, 2008, http://www.mortgagenewsdaily.com/10232000_Ratings _Agencies_.asp.

Chapter 9

1. A. L. McGill, "Context Effects in Judgments of Causation," *Journal of Personality and Social Psychology* 57, no. 2 (1989): 189–200.

2. S. Rathje, "The Danger of Searching for One True Cause," *Psychology Today,* August 19, 2019, https://www.psychologytoday.com/us/blog/words-matter/201908 /you-know-less-you-think.

3. Z. Beauchamp, "A New Study Reveals the Real Reason Voters Switched to Trump," Vox, October 16, 2018, https://www.vox.com/policy-and-politics/2018/10 /16/17980820/trump-obama-2016-race-racism-class-economy-2018-midterm.

4. T. Lombrozo, "Simplicity and Probability in Causal Explanation," *Cognitive Psychology* 55 (2007): 232–57.

5. H. Rosling, *Factfulness: Ten Reasons We're Wrong about the World* (New York: Flatiron Books, 2018).

6. N. Paharia, K. S. Kassam, J. D. Greene, and M. H. Bazerman, "Dirty Work, Clean Hands: The Moral Psychology of Indirect Agency," *Organizational Behavior and Human Decision Processes* 109, no. 2 (2009): 134–41.

7. L. C. Coffman, "Intermediation Reduces Punishment (and Reward)," *American Economic Journal: Microeconomics* 3, no. 4 (2011): 77–106.

8. D. J. Simons and C. F. Chabris, "Gorillas in Our Midst: Sustained Inattentional Blindness for Dynamic Events," *Perception* 28, no. 9 (1999): 1059–1074. See video at https://www.youtube.com/watch?v=vJG698U2Mvo.

9. A. E. Tenbrunsel and D. M. Messick, "Ethical Fading: The Role of Self-Deception in Unethical Behavior," *Social Justice Research* 17 (2004): 223–36.

10. I. Ritov and J. Baron, "Reluctance to Vaccinate: Omission Bias and Ambiguity," *Journal of Behavioral Decision Making* 3 (1990): 263–77; J. R. Meszaros, D. A. Asch, J. Baron, J. C. Hershey, H. Kunreuther, and J. Schwartz-Buzaglo, "Cognitive Processes and the Decisions of Some Parents to Forego Pertussis Vaccination for Their Children," *Journal of Clinical Epidemiology* 49 (1996): 697–703.

11. Greene, *Moral Tribes.*

12. P. Foot, *Virtues and Vices and Other Essays in Moral Philosophy* (New York: Oxford University Press, USA, 1978); Greene, *Moral Tribes.*

13. I. Kant, *Groundwork of the Metaphysics of Morals* (New York: Harper & Row, 1964).

14. M. H. Bazerman, *The Power of Noticing: What the Best Leaders See* (New York: Simon & Schuster, 2014).

15. Guiora, *Armies of Enablers.*

16. C. A. Sanderson, "Slippery Slopes and the Boiling-Frog Effect: How the Republican Party Succumbed to Trump," *USA Today*, December 23, 2020, https://www.usatoday.com/story/opinion/2020/12/23/surrender-to-donald-trump-republicans-slippery-slope-column/3989411001/.

17. Sanderson, "Slippery Slopes."

18. F. Gino and M. H. Bazerman, "When Misconduct Goes Unnoticed: The Acceptability of Gradual Erosion in Others' Unethical Behavior," *Journal of Experimental Social Psychology* 45, no. 4 (2009): 708–19.

19. M. H. Bazerman and D. Moore, *Judgment in Managerial Decision Making*, 8th ed. (New York: Wiley, 2013).

20. D. T. Welsh, L. D. Ordóñez, D. G. Snyder, and M. S. Christian, "The Slippery Slope: How Small Ethical Transgressions Pave the Way for Larger Future Transgressions," *Journal of Applied Psychology* 100, no. 1 (2015): 114–27.

21. Sanderson, "Slippery Slopes."

22. Twohey et al., "Weinstein's Complicity Machine."

23. Farrow, *Catch and Kill*, 38–39.

Chapter 10

1. G. Packer, "The President Is Winning His War on American Institutions," *Atlantic*, April 2020, https://www.theatlantic.com/magazine/archive/2020/04/how-to-destroy-a-government/606793/.

2. Packer, "President."

3. Packer, "President."

4. Packer, "President."

5. E. Newland, "I'm Haunted by What I Did as a Lawyer in the Trump Justice Department," *New York Times*, December 20, 2020, https://www.nytimes.com/2020/12/20/opinion/trump-justice-department-lawyer.html.

6. Newland, "I'm Haunted."

7. A. E. Tenbrunsel, K. A. Diekmann, K. Wade-Benzoni, and M. H. Bazerman, "The Ethical Mirage: A Temporal Explanation as to Why We Aren't as Ethical as We Think We Are," *Research in Organizational Behavior* 30 (2010): 153–73.

8. T. Rogers and M. H. Bazerman, "Future Lock-In: Future Implementation Increases Selection of 'Should' Choices," *Organizational Behavioral and Human Decision Processes* 106, no. 1 (2008): 1–20.

9. R. Fisher and W. Ury, *Getting to Yes* (New York: Penguin, 1981).

10. J. R. Detert, "Cultivating Everyday Courage," *Harvard Business Review*, November–December 2018, https://hbr.org/2018/11/cultivating-everyday-courage.

11. S. E. Asch, "Effects of Group Pressure on the Modification and Distortion of Judgments," in *Groups, Leadership and Men*, ed. H. Guetzkow (Pittsburgh: Carnegie Press, 1951), 177–90.

12. Tenbrunsel et al., "Ethical Mirage."

13. Chugh, *The Person You Mean to Be*.

14. J. Haidt, *The Righteous Mind: Why Good People Are Divided by Politics and Religion* (New York: Pantheon Books, 2012).

15. Singer, *Practical Ethics*.

16. S. Biles, "Feelings . . . ," Twitter, January 18, 2018, https://twitter.com/Simone_Biles/status/953014513837715457.

17. *Simone vs. Herself* (Facebook Watch Original), online docuseries, https://www.facebook.com/watch/vsonwatch/517934389392544/.

18. J. Macur, "Simone Biles and the Weight of Perfection," *New York Times*, July 24, 2021, https://www.nytimes.com/2021/07/24/sports/olympics/simone-biles-gymnastics.html.

19. S. Stump, "Simone Biles Returning to Olympics to Be a Voice for Abuse Survivors," The Today Show website, April 14, 2021, https://www.today.com/news/simone-biles-competing-tokyo-olympics-be-voice-abuse-survivors-t214955.

20. Macur, "Simone Biles."

21. L. Clarke, "Simone Biles Blasts USA Gymnastics' Settlement Proposal; Aly Raisman Assails 'Massive Cover Up,'" *Washington Post*, August 7, 2019, https://www.washingtonpost.com/sports/2020/02/29/simone-biles-aly-raisman-blast-usa-gymnastics-settlement-proposal/.

22. Clarke, "Simone Biles."

23. Macur, "Simone Biles."

24. S. Lewis, "Simone Biles Says She Feels the 'Weight of the World' on Her Shoulders after Tough Olympic Qualifiers," CBS News, July 26, 2021, https://www.cbsnews.com/news/simone-biles-olympics-gymnastics-qualifiers/.

25. A. North, "America's Mental Health Moment Is Finally Here," Vox, July 30, 2021, https://www.vox.com/22596341/simone-biles-withdrawal-osaka-olympics-mental-health.

26. M. Hohman, "Simone Biles Addresses for 1st Time Whether Nassar Abuse Impacted Olympics Performance," The Today Show website, August 4, 2021, https://www.today.com/news/simone-biles-nassar-abuse-s-impact-tokyo-performance-today-t227296.

27. D. Barrett, "Simone Biles to Congress: 'I Blame Larry Nassar, and I Also Blame an Entire System,'" *Washington Post*, September 15, 2021, https://www.washingtonpost.com/national-security/gymnasts-nassar-fbi-investigation-hearing/2021/09/14/de4832cc-159f-11ec-9589-31ac3173c2e5_story.html.

28. M. Luo, "Mitt Romney's Act of Political Courage," *New Yorker*, February 5, 2020, https://www.newyorker.com/news/our-columnists/mitt-romneys-act-of-political-courage.

29. John F. Kennedy Library Foundation, "U.S. Senator Mitt Romney to Receive the John F. Kennedy Profiles in Courage Award," press release, March 26, 2021, https://www.jfklibrary.org/about-us/news-and-press/press-releases/2021-profile-in-courage-award-announcement.

30. M. Romney, "Full Transcript: Mitt Romney's Speech Announcing Vote to Convict Trump," *New York Times*, February 5, 2020, https://www.nytimes.com/2020/02/05/us/politics/mitt-romney-impeachment-speech-transcript.html.

31. Luo, "Mitt Romney's Act of Political Courage."

32. Luo, "Mitt Romney's Act of Political Courage."

33. M. Leibovich, "Romney, Defying the Party He Once Personified, Votes to Convict Trump," *New York Times*, February 5, 2020, https://www.nytimes.com/2020/02/05/us/politics/romney-trump-impeachment.html.

34. John F. Kennedy Library Foundation, "U.S. Senator Mitt Romney."

35. Financial Crisis Inquiry Commission, "The Financial Crisis Inquiry Report," January 2011, https://www.govinfo.gov/content/pkg/GPO-FCIC/pdf/GPO-FCIC.pdf.

36. The Investopedia Team, "Federal Reserve Regulations," Investopedia, December 15, 2020, https://www.investopedia.com/terms/f/federal-reserve-regulations.asp.

37. J. Bernstein, "Inside the New York Fed: Secret Recordings and a Culture Clash," ProPublica, September 26, 2014, https://www.propublica.org/article/carmen-segarras-secret-recordings-from-inside-new-york-fed.

38. Bernstein, "Inside the New York Fed."

39. Bernstein, "Inside the New York Fed."

40. J. Weir, "Goldman Sachs Whistleblower Carmen Segarra Speaks Up Again," Rantt Media, October 19, 2019, https://rantt.com/goldman-sachs-whistleblower-carmen-segarra-speaks-up-again.

41. J. Bernstein, "The Secret Recordings of Carmen Segarra," *This American Life*, September 26, 2014, podcast, https://www.thisamericanlife.org/536/the-secret-recordings-of-carmen-segarra; Bernstein, "Inside the New York Fed: Secret

Recordings and a Culture Clash," ProPublica, September 26, 2014, https://www
.propublica.org/article/carmen-segarras-secret-recordings-from-inside-new-york-fed.

42. Bernstein, "Secret Recordings of Carmen Segarra."

43. Weir, "Segarra Speaks Up Again."

44. Weir, "Segarra Speaks Up Again."

45. Bernstein, "Secret Recordings of Carmen Segarra."

46. Weir, "Segarra Speaks Up Again."

47. C. Anthony, "Theranos Whistleblowers Model Courage, Integrity," McCoy
Family Center for Ethics in Society, Stanford University, February 26, 2019, https://
ethicsinsociety.stanford.edu/buzz-blog/theranos-whistleblowers-model-courage
-integrity.

48. Anthony, "Theranos Whistleblowers."

49. Anthony, "Theranos Whistleblowers."

50. Carreyrou, *Bad Blood*, 197.

51. Carreyrou, *Bad Blood*, 198.

52. T. Dunn, V. Thompson, R. Jarvis, and A. Louszko, "Ex Theranos CEO Eliza
beth Holmes Says 'I Don't Know' 600-Plus Times in Never-Before-Broadcast Deposi-
tion Tapes," ABC News, January 23, 2019, https://abcnews.go.com/Business/theranos
-ceo-elizabeth-holmes-600-times-broadcast-deposition/story?id=60576630.

53. M. H. Bazerman, *The Power of Noticing: What the Best Leaders See* (New York:
Simon & Schuster, 2014).

54. R. N. Proctor, *Golden Holocaust: Origins of the Cigarette Catastrophe and the
Case for Abolition* (Berkeley: University of California Press, 2012).

55. A. M. Brandt, *The Cigarette Century: The Rise, Fall, and Deadly Persistence of
the Product That Defined America* (Basic Books, 2007).

56. Proctor, *Golden Holocaust*.

57. Wikipedia, "Coumarin," accessed November 10, 2021, https://en.wikipedia
.org/wiki/Coumarin.

58. Goldberg Kohn Ltd., "Famous Whistleblowers and Their Impact on America,"
January 26, 2019, https://www.whistleblowersattorneys.com/blogs-whistleblower
blog,famous-whistleblowers-in-america.

59. C. Feldman, "60 Minutes' Most Famous Whistleblower," CBS News, February 4, 2016, https://www.cbsnews.com/news/60-minutes-most-famous-whistleblower/.

Chapter 11

1. D. A. Moore and M. H. Bazerman, *Decision Leadership* (New Haven, CT: Yale
University Press, 2022).

2. K. Benner, "Trump and Justice Dept. Lawyer Said to Have Plotted to Oust
Acting Attorney General," *New York Times*, October 13, 2021, https://www.nytimes
.com/2021/01/22/us/politics/jeffrey-clark-trump-justice-department-election.html.

3. Benner, "Trump and Justice Dept. Lawyer."

4. E. Bazelon and M. Wines, "How the Census Bureau Stood Up to Trump's Meddling," *New York Times*, August 15, 2021, https://www.nytimes.com/2021/08/12 /sunday-review/census-redistricting-trump-immigrants.html.

5. Bazelon and Wines, "Census Bureau."

6. H. L. Wang, "Immigration Hard-Liner Files Reveal 40-Year Bid behind Trump's Census Obsession," National Public Radio, February 15, 2021, https://www.npr.org /2021/02/15/967783477/immigration-hard-liner-files-reveal-40-year-bid-behind -trumps-census-obsession.

7. Bazelon and Wines, "Census Bureau."

8. M. L. Tushman and C. A. O'Reilly, *Winning through Innovation* (Cambridge, MA: Harvard Business School Press, 2016).

9. C. A. O'Reilly III and M. L. Tushman, *Winning Through Innovation: A Practical Guide to Leading Organizational Change and Renewal.* (Boston: Harvard Business School Press, 1997).

10. I. Ayres and C. Unkovic, "Information Escrows," *Michigan Law Review* 111, no. 2 (2012): 145–96.

11. Ayres and Unkovic, "Information Escrows."

12. C. Joffe-Walt, "Episode One: The Book of Statuses," July 30, 2020, in *Nice White Parents*, produced by J. Snyder, podcast, https://www.nytimes.com/2020/07 /30/podcasts/nice-white-parents-serial.html.

13. D. A. Moore, D. M. Cain, G. Loewenstein, and M. Bazerman, eds., *Conflicts of Interest: Problems and Solutions from Law, Medicine, and Organizational Settings* (New York: Cambridge University Press, 2005).

14. Guiora, *Armies of Enablers.*

15. Guiora, *Armies of Enablers.*

16. "What Is a Whistleblower?" Government Accountability Project, accessed November 10, 2021, https://whistleblower.org/resources/.

17. L. Herrero, "The Missing Word in the Famous Margaret Mead Quote," Leandro Herrero website, February 19, 2016, https://leandroherrero.com/the-missing-word-in -the-famous-margaret-mead-quote/.

Epilogue

1. M. H. Bazerman, *The Power of Noticing: What the Best Leaders See* (New York: Simon & Schuster, 2014).

INDEX

A NOTE ON THE TYPE

This book has been composed in Adobe Text and Gotham.
Adobe Text, designed by Robert Slimbach for Adobe,
bridges the gap between fifteenth- and sixteenth-century
calligraphic and eighteenth-century Modern styles.
Gotham, inspired by New York street signs, was designed
by Tobias Frere-Jones for Hoefler & Co.